The Teen's Steer to College and Career Planning.

Bonus :Top 15 Freshman Year Faux Pas.The Common Blunders: A Guide to Avoiding Freshman Mistakes.

By:Felicia Tree

1

Disclaimer:

The information provided in this book is for general informational purposes only. The author and publisher assume no responsibility for errors, inaccuracies, or omissions, and expressly disclaim any liability for any loss or damage incurred by any person due to the use or reliance on any information in this book. While every effort has been made to provide accurate and up-to-date information, the rapidly changing nature of personal development and time management means that the content may not always reflect the most current research or trends. This book is not intended to replace expert advice.

Readers are encouraged to seek professional guidance for their specific circumstances. The author and publisher disclaim any responsibility for actions taken by readers based on the information provided in this book. Any product or company names mentioned in this book are for identification purposes only and do not constitute an endorsement or recommendation. The views expressed by the author are solely their own and do not necessarily reflect the views of any affiliated organizations or individuals.

About The Author

 Hello, my name is Felicia Tree, and I'm thrilled to be the voice behind this book! Let me tell you a little bit about myself. I'm not your typical writer; I'm a personal development coach, and let me tell you, it's more than just a job for me; it's my heart and soul.

My journey into the area of personal development began with a genuine desire to assist individuals in living their best lives. Consider this: a blend of inspiration, a sprinkle of harsh love, and a slew of solutions for overcoming life's obstacles. That is what I bring to the table. My purpose as your personal development coach is simple: to guide you through the maze of life and assist you in mastering it. I'm not simply giving suggestions in these pages; I'm putting out a road map to help you in your career planning , create crushing goals, and genuinely grasp the "why" behind what you do. Whether you're scrolling through this on a lazy Sunday or utilising it as your daily dose of motivation, know that I'm rooting for you.

So, as you absorb the information in these chapters, keep in mind that it's not just the advice from an author - it's a conversation between friends, with me urging you towards your best self. Here's to making waves in the sea of personal development.

Table of contents.

<u>- Exploring Career Options.</u>
<u>- Understanding the Job Market.</u>
<u>- Job shadowing, internships, and volunteer opportunities.</u>

<u>Chapter 2:</u>

<u>Academic Planning and College Readiness.</u>
<u>- Creating a High School Plan That Aligns with Career Goals.</u>
<u>Understanding College Admissions Requirements.</u>
<u>- Extracurricular Activities and Their Impact on College Admissions.</u>
<u>College admissions tests (SAT, ACT, etc.).</u>

<u>Chapter 3:</u>
<u>College Research and Decision Making.</u>
<u>Types of Colleges and Degrees (Community Colleges, Universities, Vocational Schools, Online Education.</u>
<u>- Researching Colleges (using online tools and college fairs)</u>

- Applying to Colleges (application process, essays, letters of recommendation)
- Financing College (scholarships, grants, loans, work-study programs).

Chapter 4:
Career Technical Education and Alternative Paths.
- Trade Schools and Apprenticeships.
- Military Options
- Gap Year Opportunities
- Direct-to-Workforce Prospects

**Chapter 5:
Soft Skills and Personal Development**.
- Communication skills.
- Time Management.
- Teamwork and Leadership.
- Problem Solving and Critical Thinking.
- Networking and Building Professional Relationships.

**Chapter 6:
Boss Battle - Dealing with Bullies*

- **Identifying the Enemy: Recognizing Different Forms of Bullying.**
- Winning Strategies: Effective Ways to Stand Up to Bullies.
- Summoning Help: When and How to Get Adults Involved.

Chapter 7:
The Application Process (Jobs and Colleges)**
- Writing Resumes and Cover Letters.
- Filling Out Applications.
- Interview Techniques and Practice.
- Follow-Up and Thank You Notes.
- Make it brief but meaningful.

Chapter 8
: Financial Literacy and Management.**
- Budgeting for Teens
Understanding Student Loans and Debt.
- Saving and Investing
- Managing a Bank Account.

Chapter 9:

<u>Conclusion</u>
<u>I HAVE A REQUEST</u>
<u>Additional Resources.</u>

Introduction

Congratulations, Are you at the crossroads of high school, looking into the exciting yet perplexing future of college and career options? Fasten your seatbelts, because "Teens' Guide to College and Career Planning" is your definitive guide through this thrilling adventure! Consider this book your own mentor, a guiding light through the murk of PSATs, majors, resumes, and job interviews. This guide is about more than simply getting into your dream college; it is also about writing the first chapter of your success story. As you go through these pages, you'll go from being a perplexed high school student to a confident navigator of your future. Let's go on this adventure together, deciphering the secrets of adulthood and forging a path to the future you've always wanted!

The Importance of Early Planning

As a teenager, early planning is similar to creating a road map for your journey. It may appear that there is plenty of time to work things out, but just as when planning a trip, knowing your destination ahead of time can make everything go more smoothly. Here's why it matters:

1. **Goal Setting:** Planning helps you choose what you want to accomplish. Setting goals, like picking what game to play or what movie to watch, provides you with something to aspire towards.

2) **Time Management:** Time is like pocket money; use it wisely and you will get more out of it. When you plan ahead of time, you learn to make the most use of your time, setting aside some for fun and some for business.

3. **Reduced Stress:** Have you ever been panicked because you waited until the last minute to do your homework? Early planning for

larger events, such as your future profession or education, reduces last-minute stress.

4. **Make Better Decisions:** Planning is like to using a torch in the dark: it allows you to see and avoid obstacles and wrong turns. With a strategy, you're less likely to make decisions you'll regret later.

5. **Learning Opportunities:** When you start preparing, you typically discover that you require specific talents or information. You have time to learn these, just like you would study a new game before becoming proficient at it.

6. **Adapting to Change:** Things change; perhaps you'll enjoy something new, or an opportunity arises. A plan allows you to adjust more quickly, such as changing characters in a game while still knowing how to play.

7. **Boosting Confidence:** When you plan and track your progress, it's like levelling up in a game. You have more confidence in your talents.

8. **Life Skill:** Planning teaches you abilities that you'll always need, such as thinking ahead and organising. It's like learning to ride a bike: if you master it, you'll use it all the time.

Remember, early preparation does not imply that you have everything sorted out right now. It entails starting to consider what you might like to achieve, establishing a few goals, and then taking actions towards them. It's like drawing a map with a pencil; you can always make changes as you go!

How to Use This Guide

To get the most out of this guide, use a step-by-step approach:

Step 1: Get acquainted with the guide's structure.

First, skim through the guide to get a sense of how it is organised. Look for headings, subheadings, bullet points, and highlighted material. These characteristics frequently identify the primary issues and essential points, allowing you to predict the types of material you'll encounter.

Step 2: Define Your Objective
Ask yourself what you hope to accomplish by reading this guide. Perhaps you are looking for specific information, trying to acquire a new skill, or simply surfing to broaden your knowledge. Having a specific aim in mind will allow you to focus on the areas that are important to your needs.

Step 3: Review the material
If the handbook has a table of contents, utilise it to find the portions most relevant to your aims. This saves time and prevents you from becoming distracted by less relevant stuff.

Step 4: Actively engage with the material.
As you read, interact with the text rather than passively absorbing it. Take notes, ask questions, and try to relate the new material to what you

already know. This will aid with retention and comprehension.

Step 5: Use the information practically
If the material is instructional, use the instructions or advice as practically as possible. Whether it's a software guide or physical task instructions, repeating the steps in real-world circumstances will help you understand and recall the procedure better.

Step 6: Reflect on what you've learnt.
After you've completed the guide, take a moment to consider the important points and their ramifications. Try to summarise the important themes in your own words, and think about how you may apply this knowledge to your everyday activities or long-term ambitions.

Step 7: Refer to the guide.
Keep the instructions nearby for future reference. As you begin to apply what you've learned, you may discover that you need to revisit some portions again. Revisiting the topic

might help you solidify your understanding and verify you haven't overlooked any details.

Step 8: Seek additional resources if needed.
If the guide does not entirely address your questions, or if you want to learn more about a topic, look for additional resources such as books, websites, or professional advice.

Bonus Tips: - **Highlight or Bookmark**: Make a note of any key passages or themes you'd like to review later.
-

 Discussion with others: Explaining the topic to another person can help you grasp it better.
-

 Remain curious: Allow your discoveries to prompt other questions and inquiries.

By following these steps, you will maximise the benefits of this guide and guarantee that you not only absorb but also use the material successfully.

<u>Bonus.</u>

Top 15 Freshman Year Faux Pas**

- The Common Blunders: A Guide to Avoiding Freshman Mistakes.

Without a doubt, the transition from high school to college is a watershed moment in one's life, presenting new challenges and possibilities. To help you get through this exciting time, here's a quick guide to avoiding some common freshman mistakes:

#1: Overscheduling Yourself

Blunder: Overcommitting to multiple activities, clubs, or courses.
Avoidance Strategy: Maintain a balanced schedule. Choose a manageable course load and limit extracurricular activities, particularly during the first semester.

2. Ignoring health and sleep.

Blunder: Sacrificing sleep for socializing or studying and neglecting healthy eating and exercise.
   Avoidance Strategy: Prioritize a regular sleep schedule, eat balanced meals, and set aside time for physical activity.

3. Mismanagement of finances

To avoid financial stress, create a budget, track spending, and be mindful of purchases.

4. Skipping Class

Blunder: Failure to attend classes due to lack of enforcement.
  Avoidance Strategy: Attend all classes and take detailed notes. Remember: you are paying for these lessons!

5. Poor time management.

Blunder: Procrastinating and cramming for exams.
Avoidance Strategy: Set aside time to study for each class using a planner or digital calendar. Divide tasks into small, manageable chunks.

6. Underutilised Resources

Blunder: Not seeking assistance with coursework or personal issues.
Avoidance Strategy: Utilise campus resources like tutoring centres, libraries, academic advisors, and counselling services.

7. Forgetting to network

Blunder: Failing to connect with peers, professors, and industry professionals.

Avoidance Strategy: Participate in clubs, networking events, and class discussions to foster meaningful relationships.

8. Not backing up work.

To avoid losing important papers or projects due to technology failures, it's recommended to save work in multiple locations such as cloud storage, external drives, or flash drives.

9. Influenced by peer pressure

Blunder: Making decisions based on others' actions rather than your own.
Avoidance Strategy: Focus on your values and goals. It's acceptable to say no and make decisions that promote your well-being.

10. Selecting the incorrect course or major.

Blunder: Choosing a major without conducting adequate research or because someone else thinks it's a good idea.
Avoidance Strategy: Look into different classes and seek advice from academic advisors. Choose a major that matches your interests and strengths.

11 Lack of Adaptability

Blunder: Avoiding new experiences and failing to adapt to changing circumstances. **Avoidance Strategy**: Be open to new ideas, people, and experiences. Adaptability is critical to college success.

12: Overcommitting to Relationships

Blunder: Prioritising a relationship over academics and social life.
Avoidance Strategy: Balance time between relationships, studies, and socialising with others.

13. Disregarding Personal Safety

Blunder: Failure to prioritise personal security on campus.
Avoidance Strategy: Utilise campus escort services at night and stay alert to your surroundings.

14. Falling behind in classwork

Blunder: Allowing assignments to pile up until they become overwhelming.
Avoidance Strategy: Keep up with your workload by doing a little every day rather than waiting until the last minute.

15: Not Being Yourself

Blunder: Trying to reinvent yourself to the point where you feel inauthentic.

Avoidance Strategy: Value your individuality while remaining open to growth and change.

Remember that making mistakes is a normal part of the learning process, particularly during your freshman year. The key is to be aware, learn from them, and make changes as you go. College is an excellent opportunity to learn more about yourself, what you want out of life, and lay the groundwork for your future. Keep these suggestions in mind, and don't forget to enjoy the journey!

- Social Side Quests: Navigating Cliques and New Friendships.

As a teenager, social side quests can be just as exciting and rewarding as any video game or fantasy quest. Here's a guide to navigating cliques and making new friends, divided into simple "quests" for you to complete.

Quest 1: Reconnaissance Mission
Objective: Identify the various types of cliques in your environment.

1. **Watch and Learn**: Take some time to quietly observe the various groups around you. Consider what they talk about, what they wear, and what activities they enjoy.
2. Identify the Lay of the Land: Recognise that every clique has its own "culture" and norms. Make a mental note of these distinctions; they will be useful later.

Quest 2: Common Ground Exploration
Objective: Find something in common with people from various cliques.

1. **Discover Shared Interests**: Look for topics that you genuinely care about and that members of the clique do as well. It could be music, sports, video games, or movies.
2. **Engage Casually**: Start light conversations about your common interests without trying too hard to fit in right away. Your genuine interest is the key.

Quest 3: The Solo Avatar Upgrade.

Objective: Gain confidence and pursue your own interests.

1. **Skill Acquisition**: Begin a new hobby or learn something new that interests you. This will not only boost your confidence, but may also pique the interest of like-minded peers.
2. **Self-Empowerment**: Practice self-affirmation and goal setting. People gravitate towards those who are at ease with themselves.

Quest 4: First Contact Initiative
Objective: Take the first step towards forming a new friendship.

1. **Small Quests**: Begin by performing small, friendly acts for others, such as assisting with homework or providing a genuine compliment.
2. **Invite Participation**: Suggest a group activity based on your shared interests, such as a study session or a pick-up basketball game.

Quest 5: The Diversification Endeavour
Objective: Expand your network and connect
with people from various cliques.

1. **Mix and Match**: Accept invitations from
various groups or invite someone from another
clique to participate in your activities.
2. **Respect Boundaries**: Recognise that not
everyone may be willing to mix cliques. Respect
others' boundaries in the same way that you want
your own to be respected.

Quest Six: The Friendship Forge
Goal: Develop newly formed connections into
friendships.

1. **One-on-One Interactions**: Spend time
with your new acquaintances outside of larger
group settings.
2. **Listen and Support**: Foster a deeper
connection by listening to and supporting others.

Quest 7: Resilience Rally

Objective: Respond positively to rejections and setbacks.

1. **Shrug Off Rejection**: If someone does not want to be friends, do not take it personally. There are many others who will be.
2. **Reflect and Adapt**: Use your negative experiences to learn and grow. Consider how you approach people and what you might do differently the next time.

Quest 8: Inner Circle Campaign
Objective: Build a circle of friends who value you.

1. **Quality over Quantity**: Prioritise developing friendships with people who value you for who you are, rather than the clique to which you belong.
2. **Maintain and Nurture**: Consistently invest in these friendships with time, effort, and genuine concern.

Remember, the goal of these social side quests isn't to be the most popular or to fit in with a specific group, but to make meaningful connections and enjoy your teenage social life!

Chapter 1:

Self-Assessment and Career Exploration**

Self-assessments are an excellent tool to evaluate your job performance and identify areas for improvement. You can tailor self-assessments to incorporate the characteristics that are most relevant to your life and career. If you're preparing for the future or setting new goals, reflecting on your skills, shortcomings, values, and accomplishments might help you figure out what to work on next.

Identifying Your Interests, Skills, and Values

Identifying your interests, skills, and values is an important step in better understanding yourself and making decisions about your future. As a teenager, you're still figuring out what makes you tick. Here's a quick guide to help you through the discovery phase:

Identifying Your Interests

Explore New Activities: - Join clubs or groups at school or in your neighbourhood.
- Attend workshops or classes on a variety of topics that interest you.
- Participate in various sports, arts, and voluntary activity.

Reflect on Past Enjoyment:
- Think about the activities you enjoyed as a child. Are you still interested?
- Recall any projects or chores that you lost track of time doing.

Ask yourself:
- What topics do you love reading and learning about?
- What do you daydream about?

35

- Are there any TV shows, books, or films that enthral you?

Identify Your Skills:

Self-Reflection:
- Consider your strengths based on feedback from friends and family.
- Consider which courses in school come readily to you.

Experimentation:
- Identify successful talents from school projects or part-time work.
- Experiment with several skills, such as writing and art, coding, and public speaking, to determine your strengths.

Feedback:
- Ask teachers, friends, and family for feedback on your strengths.
- Seek constructive feedback to better understand your skills.

Identifying your values:

Consider Your Perfect Day: Imagine an ideal day. Who are you with? What are you doing now? This could reflect your values.

Think about the big picture:
- What issues in the world are you concerned about?
- What causes you to feel proud?
- When did you feel the happiest and most fulfilled?

Create a list of attributes you like in others, such as honesty, inventiveness, and determination. These frequently represent your personal values.

Evaluate Decisions:
- Consider past decisions that seemed right. What principles were you upholding with those choices?

Visualisation:

- Picture yourself in the future. What kind of person would you like to be? What aspects of your lifestyle and job cannot be compromised?

Try Assessments:
- Online quizzes and assessments might assist determine your core values.

Putting It All Together:

After spending some time researching these areas:

1. Look for patterns: Are there any activities or themes that consistently appear in your interests and skills?

2. Prioritise: Choose the top five most significant interests, talents, and values from the list you've created.

3. Look into occupations and hobbies that are compatible with your top interests, abilities, and beliefs.

4. Set goals to improve your talents and participate more with your interests.

5. Review and update your lists on a regular basis; they may change as you expand.

Remember, discovering your interests, abilities, and values is an ongoing process. What thrills and motivates you now may change as you gain new experiences and insights. Keep an open mind and be gentle with yourself as you embark on this personal discovery trip.

Tools for Self-Assessment (career quizzes, aptitude tests, etc.)

Absolutely! As a kid, contemplating your future career may be both exhilarating and overwhelming. But do not worry! There are some useful tools available to assist you discover more about yourself and what career path would be best for you. Here are a few simple self-assessment tools:

****1. Career Quiz:****

These are enjoyable, fast exams that can be found online. They ask you about your interests, favourite school courses, and hobbies. When you're finished, they'll offer occupations that might suit your interests. It's like talking to a super-intelligent computer about your future job! Examples include the MyNextMove Interest Profiler, 123 Career Test, and Career Explorer Quiz.

2. Aptitude Tests:

Aptitude tests are slightly more serious. They assess your abilities in a variety of areas, including word puzzles, numerical problems, and shapes (similar to those used in IQ tests). This might help you choose what type of work you would be interested in, such as writing, arithmetic, or visual skills.

Examples include JobTestPrep's free aptitude test and Princeton Review's career quiz.

3. Personality Type Assessment:

These evaluations help you learn more about how you connect with others, how you prefer to work, and which environments could be best for you. For example, some people thrive in groups, while others prefer to work independently. Some people prefer explicit regulations, while others prefer to make their own rules as they go.

Examples include the Myers-Briggs Type Indicator (16 Personalities) and the Big Five Personality Test.

4. Tools for Skill Assessment:

Skill assessments can help you determine what you're strong at. Perhaps you have a talent for programming code, creating art, assisting others with problems, or organising events. These programmes frequently provide a list of talents and ask you to rate yourself on them.

Examples include SkillsYouNeed.com's Personal SWOT Analysis and MindTools Skill Assessment.

5. Career Exploration Sites:
Some websites combine quizzes, aptitude tests, and helpful information to help you explore various career possibilities. They may also show you what type of schooling or training you will need for various occupations.
Examples:
- CareerOneStop.org - Bureau of Labour Statistics' Occupational Outlook Handbook.

Protips for Using These Tools:

- Have fun with this! Do not take the results too seriously; they are simply suggestions to help you consider your options.
- Try multiple tools to gain a comprehensive view of your options.

- Discuss your results with family, instructors, or career counsellors who can provide additional insight.

- Remember that your hobbies and skills may evolve and change over time, so what appears to be a good fit today may be different in a few years.

- Finally, consider these tools to be the start of your trip rather than the end. They're here to help you generate ideas and ask the proper questions about your future.

- Exploring Career Options.

Career exploration can help you figure out your next steps, whether you're a recent graduate looking for work or you're already in a job but considering a change. Career exploration can also help you gain confidence, which will impress a hiring manager, and make relationships with people in different fields.

What is career exploration?

Career exploration occurs once you have a deeper understanding of your personality, values, talents, and interests. It requires systematically reviewing a list of jobs that are a good fit for you and conducting research to learn more about that career path. As you go, you'll see that some occupations better match your hobbies, while others may have a lengthier career path that allows you to develop your talents and receive promotions.

The purpose of job exploration is to conduct research to understand more about your alternatives and reduce them down to one career path that best fits you. By constantly assessing where you are in your job, if you are happy, and how to achieve a more rewarding career, you will learn more about yourself as well as new concepts and abilities.

 Here's a quick guide to get you started:

1. **Identify Your Interests**: Consider what you enjoy to do in your leisure time. Do you enjoy working on computers, reading, painting, or participating in sports? Your hobbies can provide insight into future vocations.

2. **Assess Your Skills**: Are you particularly good in arithmetic, writing, or public speaking? Make a list of your abilities and consider professions that might require them.

3. **Explore Careers**: Look up various job types online, read about them, watch videos, or visit career exploration websites. Learn what people in those positions do on a daily basis.

4. **Talk to People**: Engage in conversations with adults from various occupations. Ask them what they enjoy and hate about their careers, as well as any advice they have for someone just starting out.

5. **Part-Time Jobs and Internships**: If you're old enough, look into part-time work or

internships. It's an excellent method to obtain work experience while also experimenting in a new profession.

6. **Volunteer**: Volunteering can help you develop skills and gain experience in a variety of professional contexts.

7. **Use Career Surveys**: Some schools offer career surveys or inventories that might recommend careers based on your interests and abilities.

8. **Join School groups**: Get involved in groups or teams that are relevant to your possible professional path. They can provide insight and experience in a variety of fields.

9. **Educational Electives**: Choose electives at school that are relevant to careers you are interested in. If you think you might enjoy engineering, consider taking a drawing or robotics class.

10. **Make a Plan**: Once you've come up with some ideas, consider what you'll need to do to get there. Which topics should you focus on? Do you need more schooling after high school?

11. **Remain open-minded**: Your hobbies may shift as you learn and grow, and that's fine! Be open to trying new things and changing your ideas.

12. **Set Goals**: Setting goals can help you focus your exploration. They can be short-term, like joining a new club, or long-term, like pursuing a specific college degree.

Finally, keep in mind that you do not have to pursue a career on your own. Friends, family, instructors, and counsellors can all be part of your trip, offering encouragement and advice along the way. Enjoy the process and do not rush. You have plenty of time to determine the best course for you.

- **Understanding the Job Market.**

Hey, there! Diving into the job market may feel similar to climbing onto a large, twisty slide at the playground—exciting but also dangerous, right? But do not worry! I'll break it down into simple steps so you can understand how everything works.

What is the Job Market, Anyway?

Consider the job market to be a large shopping mall where, instead of purchasing clothes or gadgets, businesses are seeking for people with certain abilities to accomplish jobs, and individuals like you are looking for positions that match their skills and interests. It's a hectic environment where jobs are the "products," and they come in a variety of shapes and sizes.

Sure, let's define the job market in simple terms.

Think of the employment market as a large supermarket.

- **Shelves for Jobs:** In a supermarket, you will see shelves full of various things. In the employment market, instead of groceries, there are various types of jobs. Jobs, like fruits, vegetables, and snacks, are classified into categories such as technology, healthcare, and teaching.

- **People looking for jobs:** People looking for work are similar to grocery customers. They have a list of what they want from a job, such as how much money they want to make (income), what they're strong at (skills), and the type of work they want to accomplish (interests).

- **Businesses Seeking Workers:** Businesses look for the greatest individuals to hire, just as you would look for the best apples or cookies. They also have a list of things they seek, such as specific abilities, experience, and the type of school or training a person has.

How This Works:

1. **Supplies and Demand:** In layman's terms, when many firms require workers and there aren't enough people looking for employment, job searchers benefit (they have more options and can negotiate better compensation). However, if there are many individuals looking for employment and not enough jobs available, finding work might be difficult, and salaries may be lower. That's supply and demand.

2. Changes in the market: Just as fashion and technology change, so does the work market. positions can become popular and more lucrative if they are in high demand (for example, coding positions when a new technology is released), or they can disappear if they are no longer required.

3. **Education and Training Matters:** Many vocations require unique abilities, just as some

recipes call for specific ingredients. Obtaining the necessary education, training, or experience is similar to ensuring that you have all of the elements to prepare for the desired profession.

4. **Location, Location:** Jobs are not the same everywhere. particular foods are easier to find in particular regions (for example, seafood near the beach), and certain vocations are more popular in certain places due to the industries that exist. For example, technology employment may be more available in Silicon Valley.

5. **Getting The Job:** Finding work is similar to going grocery shopping. You might have to wait in line (complete the application procedure), speak with the cashier (attend an interview) and pay for your groceries (accept the job and the compensation offered). If everything checks out, you can take your groceries home—or, in career terms, you're employed!

Remember that, like any market, the employment market can appear complex, but it is just about matching what people can accomplish with what businesses require. Keep an eye on how the market changes in response to trends, technology, and other factors so that you can be in the right place at the right time.

Understand What You Are 'Selling'

Before you can secure a job, you must first identify your strengths. Are you great at organising things? Maybe you're amazing with animals or can explain maths problems to your buddies. All of these skills could be valuable in the workplace. Consider your abilities, personality, and interests as 'goods' to offer in the employment market.

Job Options for Teenagers

As a teenager, your work opportunities may differ from those of adults. There are a few types:

1. **Part-time Jobs:** Examples include working a few hours after school or on weekends. Think about retail stores, quick food eateries, or tutoring.

2. **Summer Jobs:** Jobs during summer vacation, such as lifeguarding at a pool, working at a camp, or assisting at a local business.

3. ** Internships:** These are essentially sneak peaks into a career, where you work with pros and learn on the job. They are frequently seen in offices or businesses.

4. **Apprenticeships:** They combine work and study, making them ideal for those who enjoy getting their hands dirty while learning valuable skills, such as carpentry or mechanics.

How to Find Job Listings

The employment market includes a lot of venues to seek for job openings.

- **Online job boards:** Indeed, Monster, and Snagajob are examples of large bulletin boards containing job advertising for a variety of positions.

- **Local Business:** When you walk past a shop or restaurant, you may notice a "Help Wanted" sign in the window.

- **School Career Centres:** Some colleges provide a person or office who can assist students in finding work and provide job search advice.

- *Social media:** Websites such as LinkedIn can be valuable, and simply telling friends and family that you're seeking for work can lead to prospects.

Building Your Resume

Your resume functions as a self-promotion tool. It includes a summary of your talents, experiences, and personal information. Even if you haven't worked before, you can mention:

- **Volunteer Work:** Anything you've done for free, such as helping out at a charity event.

- **School Clubs:** Participating in school groups or athletics demonstrates your teamwork and motivation.

- **undertakings or Hobbies:** Any unique undertakings, such as a lemonade stand or a technology project, demonstrate your initiative and passion.

Applying for Jobs

When you locate a job that sounds interesting, you'll normally need to fill out an application form or send your CV along with a cover letter, which is a brief statement describing why you're the best candidate for the position.

Interviews.

If a company believes you'd be a good fit, they will ask you to an interview. Consider it a meet-and-greet in which they ask you questions to learn more about you and determine how you would fit into their team.

Keep It Flexible.

Remember, your first work does not have to be your ideal employment. It is a beginning point. You'll learn a lot, including how to collaborate with others, handle money, and deal with real-world problems.

Safety first

Make sure you understand the labour laws for teenagers. To keep you safe and healthy, there are limits on the number of hours you can work and the kind of jobs you can undertake.

Do not get discouraged.

It is totally typical not to receive the first (or second, or third) job you apply for. Each try is good practice and brings you closer to saying "Yes!"

And that's a basic overview of the work market for teenagers. Have fun, stay interested, and good luck!

- Job shadowing, internships, and volunteer opportunities.

Let us go down these three possibilities to develop experience and abilities.

Shadowing:

- **What is it?** Shadowing is the practice of following a professional in their workplace to learn about their day-to-day responsibilities.
- **Purpose:** It allows you to gain direct experience with a specific job or vocation.
- **How it works:** You mainly just watch and learn; there isn't much hands-on activity.
- **Benefits:** It's an excellent method to gain a real-world perspective on a job without committing. It can help you determine whether you want to pursue that professional route.
- **Finding Opportunities:** You can shadow someone by asking family friends, school counsellors, or contacting nearby businesses.

Internships:

- **What is this?** An internship is a temporary assignment that provides practical experience in a job or profession.
- **Purpose:** It is intended to teach you about the field you are interested in, and it may be compensated or for school credit.
- **How does it work?** As an intern, you are expected to complete work pertaining to your topic of interest, which might range from easy to difficult.
- **Benefits:** Internships can help you gain a better understanding of a career, improve a résumé, and even lead to a job in the future.
- **Finding Opportunities:** Look via employment boards, corporate websites, school career centres, or ask your friends and relatives.

**Volunteer Opportunities:

- **What is it?** Volunteering is the act of offering your time to a non-profit, community organisation, or a cause that is important to you.
- **Purpose:** It is about giving back and, in many cases, assisting those in need.
- **How it works:** Depending on the organisation, this could include anything from volunteering at local events to working in a charity shop.
- **Benefits:** Volunteering can offer you a sense of accomplishment, teach you new skills, and improve your résumé.
- **Finding Opportunities:** Look for local charities, community centres, or internet platforms that connect volunteers to initiatives.

Remember, whether you're shadowing, interning, or volunteering, the goal is to learn and grow. Begin by considering what you enjoy or what career you might want to pursue, and then seek out opportunities in that field. Good luck!

Chapter 2:

Academic Planning and College Readiness.

Academic planning is the act of developing a four-year plan by deliberately deciding "what to learn" and "why I learn". Your plan will include scheduling your classes each semester, possibly engaging in Study Abroad programmes, choosing on a major, and completing your senior thesis. Participate in a variety of courses and extracurricular activities, set high goals, and look for your purpose for post-graduate plans as you develop a successful academic career. And college preparation or readiness You might be surprised to find that more than half of first-year college students believe they are unprepared for college, while being academically qualified.

College preparation or readiness prevent this from happening.

College preparedness is defined as the set of abilities, behaviours, and knowledge that a high school student should possess before beginning their first year of college. Counsellors and teachers play an important role in ensuring this happens and can assist students in achieving academic success in college. If you are already a teacher or are training to become one, you should understand how to best prepare your pupils for college.

- Creating a High School Plan That Aligns with Career Goals.

Creating a high school plan that corresponds with your career aspirations is similar to making your own adventure map. Like any wise explorer, you want to ensure that your map gets you directly to the treasure—your ideal job. It doesn't have to be hard; just follow these basic steps to plot your course:

Step 1: Identify Your Destination

.Before going on any journey, you must first choose a destination.Ask yourself questions such as:

- What are my interests?
- What subjects do I appreciate the most?
- What type of employment do I see myself doing in the future?
- Are there any occupations that interest me?

Once you have a basic sense of your interests and prospective future paths, you can start planning your high school experience to support those objectives.

Step 2: Gather your tools.

You'll need the correct tools, just like a compass and a map, to keep on track with your career path. These may include:

- **Guidance Counsellors:** They're similar to your navigation stars. Check in with them on a regular basis to explore your job objectives and receive advise on which courses to take.
- **Career Assessment:** These are quizzes that can help you better understand your strengths and potential occupations.
• **Internet Research:** Use the internet to learn about various careers, education requirements, and future job prospects.

Step 3: Select Your Courses Wisely

Your high school classes are the stepping stones on your path. To ensure they guide you towards your career goals, consider:

- **Core topics:** Concentrate on the core topics (such as English, math, and sciences) that are applicable to your preferred job field. For example, if you want to be an engineer, you should take more advanced math and science classes.

- **Electives**: Choose electives that will teach you skills or knowledge relevant to your professional interests. For example, if you are interested in graphic design, consider taking painting or computer graphics classes.

- **Advanced Placement (AP) or Dual Enrollment**: These can prepare you for college-level work and may even get you college credit, saving you time and money in the long run.

Step 4: Gain Experience.

Simply reading about a location is not the same as seeing it. The same applies to careers:

- **Internships or Job Shadowing:** Seek out opportunities to observe or work in your subject of interest.

- **Clubs and Organisations:** Join school clubs or local organisations that are relevant to your professional path. For example, if you're

interested in business, look for DECA or Future Business Leaders of America.
- **Volunteering:** This can help you gain hands-on experience and create a network of contacts.

Step 5: Establish Milestones

Create milestones along the journey to keep you on track:

- **Short-Term Goals:** Examples include maintaining a set GPA, taking specific classes by junior year, and joining a club each year.
- **Long-term objectives:** Consider where you want to be after you graduate, whether that's being accepted into a specific college programme or having a portfolio of your work.

Step 6: Adjust Your Route As Needed

Remember that sometimes highways are closed, or you find a more scenic path. It's okay to rethink and change your plan:

- **Be Flexible:** If you discover a new interest, modify your plan to accommodate it.
- **Ask for feedback:** Talk to teachers, mentors, and professionals in your career sector of interest to gain guidance and make informed decisions.

Step 7: Enjoy the journey.

Your high school years are more than just a sprint to the finish line. Make sure you enjoy the journey by:

- **Balancing:** Maintain a balance of academics, extracurricular activities, and downtime.
- **Reflecting:** Take the time to consider your experiences and what they have taught you about your interests and skills.

Creating a high school plan that corresponds with your career aspirations entails determining where you want to go and outlining the steps to get there. Begin simply, keep focused, and be prepared to explore new pathways along the way. Your career journey awaits!

Understanding College Admissions Requirements.

Each school has its own application requirements. These may differ for students applying directly out of high school, those wishing to transfer into a programme, and those returning to school after taking a break. Depending on your chosen major or programme, you may be required to submit additional paperwork, conduct an interview, or perform an audition. Most colleges disclose their application criteria on their websites, allowing you to begin gathering materials early. Remember that if you leave anything out of your application, you will not be considered for admission. Getting into college can feel like a daunting task, but it doesn't have to be! Consider it similar to unlocking a new level in a game that requires you to collect specific keys to enter. Here's how to nail down the basics:

1. **Grades are extremely important:**

The first key is your grades. Doing well in high school is quite crucial. Colleges look at your grades to determine how well you did in class. They don't expect you to be perfect, but they do want to see hard work and progress. If you struggled at first then improved, that's great news for you!

2. **The Tough Classes Show You Are Serious:**

Are you enrolled in challenging classes such as AP or honours? These function as power-ups for your application. .Colleges want to know that you are willing to challenge yourself.

3. **Standardised Test Scores (Sometimes)

These are your SATs or ACTs. Some institutions no longer need them (they are "test-optional"), but many still want to see how you perform. Consider these assessments to be the same level at which everyone must compete, allowing universities to compare pupils from various high schools.

4. **Extracurricular Quest:**

This is the exciting phase when you can show off what you do outside of the classroom. Sports, groups, and volunteering all provide colleges with insight into who you are and what you enjoy. They are similar to side quests that demonstrate your character's overall development.

5. **The Power of Essays:**

Your college essay allows you to talk directly to admissions officers. This is your opportunity to tell your narrative, share your successes and failures, and show them what makes you, well, you. It is beneficial to add personality to your scores and marks.

6. **Letters of recommendation:**

Think of them as character references. Teachers, coaches, and counsellors can write on how amazing you are. Choose those who know you well and can provide interesting anecdotes about your accomplishments and growth.

7. **Demonstrated Interest:**

Demonstrate your enthusiasm for the college! Visit if possible, speak with admissions representatives, or attend college fairs. This demonstrates that you sincerely want to be a part of their world.

8. Financial aid forms:

The truth is that education can be expensive, so you'll probably need some assistance paying for it. Forms such as the FAFSA or CSS Profile inform institutions that you require financial help. Treat these as treasure maps that will guide you to the gold needed to fuel your adventure.

Here's a good tip:

start getting these keys as soon as possible. Don't wait until the last minute because some things, such as academics and extracurricular activities, require time to accumulate. Remember that if you have any questions or feel lost, there are counsellors, professors, and college admissions representatives who may serve as guides on this voyage.

Let's me explain Understanding College Admissions Requirements.In depths

When reviewing the school's application criteria, pay special attention to the instructions for sending your materials. Some colleges demand applications to be submitted online, while others prefer paper applications received by postal service. If you're applying online, be sure you have a secure internet connection and are prepared to pay the application cost when the time comes to submit. If you're applying by mail, you'll need to print an application and send it in with your essential materials and a cheque. (Fee exemptions are available for qualifying students.)

What materials are necessary to complete an application?

The lists below should give you an understanding of the general application requirements, as well as what differs for transfer, returning, and adult applicants.

For First-Time College Applicants:
- Application form containing your essential personal information (name, address, contact information, family information, and previous school experience)
- Results from the SAT, ACT, and/or SAT Subject Tests
- Personal Essay
- Recommendations from teachers or counsellors
- High school transcripts.
- Responses to short answer questions
- Résumé or activity sheet
- Interview

- Additional writing samples are sought by the university.
- Portfolio or creative sample (programmes in fine art, design, film, audio, and creative writing)
- Audition (Performing Arts Programmes)

For transfer applicants:

Generally, transfer applicants must submit the same materials as first-time college applicants. However, the application process and required materials may differ in various ways.

Depending on how many college hours you've earned, you may need to apply as a transfer student or a freshman. If you have finished more than a year of college, you will most likely be a transfer student and may be required to complete a transfer application. If you have less than a year of college experience, you may need to apply as a first-time student. If this is the case, look into your prospective school's credit transfer policies. Some of your completed credits may transfer with you.

You may not have to submit your SAT, ACT, or SAT. Subject Test scores vary according on how much college-level coursework you have completed and the type of university you attended.

If necessary, include transcripts from your previous postsecondary institution(s) as well as your high school.

Letters of recommendation should be from your college teachers, dean, or adviser. Your prospective institution may specify who should provide recommendations. As a transfer student, submitting references from college instructors is preferable than contacting old high school teachers or guidance counsellors.

For returning or adult students:
With few exceptions, you will be required to submit the same paperwork as first-time college applicants.

Please submit your high school transcripts or high school equivalency certificate, as well as transcripts from any tertiary institutions you have attended.

Depending on your age, the length of time you've been out of school, and your institution, you may not be required to submit any standardised test scores with your application. To learn more about taking standardised tests as an adult, go here.

Letters of recommendation should come from someone who understand your academic goals and potential. This could be your old job, a former teacher (depending on how long you've been out of school), or another person.

What should I check for when reading the application requirements?

Deadlines: Take note of the early and regular admissions deadlines, as well as any institutional scholarships for which you may be eligible.

Application platform participation: Over 800 colleges use the Common Application, although others use the Coalition or Universal College Application. Others may request that applicants apply for admission using the school's website or a hardcopy application. Regardless of the application format, keep track of any additional materials that each institution requires as part of their application.

Transcripts: As a high school student, obtaining a transcript from your high school is too simple. Consult your guidance counsellor, and have them send an official copy to your preferred university on your behalf. As a transfer applicant or a returning or adult student, receiving your high school transcripts may be a little difficult. First, visit your high school's website to see if there is any information for alumni. If it doesn't work, phone the school to inquire about transcript services. If your school no longer exists, you should contact your state's Department of Education. Transfer, returning, or adult students who have completed some postsecondary education must additionally submit official transcripts from each college they attended. Be advised that some universities may charge a fee to locate and distribute your transcript.

Letter of Recommendation Instructions: Some schools will state that they desire recommendations from certain personnel, for example a core subject teacher, a counselor, or an adviser. Before asking someone to write you a letter, make sure you understand the requirements and how to send it to the school. Can writers submit recommendations online? Is it necessary for the writer to sign their name over the envelope seal if they are sent via postal service? Are there any specific recommendation forms to fill out?

Format for supplementary materials: Is there a certain structure for submitting your résumé, activity sheet, portfolio, creative piece, or writing sample? Were you given a prompt? Should these materials be submitted online or by mail?

Interview or audition scheduling: How is the interview or audition scheduled? Do you have to come to campus, or does the institution conduct interviews and auditions elsewhere or over

Skype? Are there set days for interviews and auditions? What should you do to prepare for your audition? Does the school provide a list of interview questions with which you should be familiar?

Test Score Practices:

Test code: Discover each school's exam code. You'll need it to submit a SAT or ACT score report to a school.

Does the college allow you to submit ACT or SAT superscores? If you have taken a test more than once, your superscore is generated by adding your highest scores from each portion of the test. To get your SAT superscore, add your greatest math score to your highest evidence-based reading and writing score. To get your ACT superscore, take the average of your greatest science, math, English, and reading scores.

All score reports Does the institution need you to submit SAT or ACT scores from each time you take them? If so, you should avoid taking either test "as practice" or for a second time without studying, as those scores will also be considered when making an admissions decision.

SAT Score Choice: Does the school allow you to submit a specific SAT or SAT Subject Test score report? If so, you may retake the test as many times as you like. Keep in mind, however, that if you decide to apply to another school later on, that institution may want a report of all of your scores.

Advanced Placement and International Baccalaureate Tests: If your school is part of the AP or IB programme, you may have had the option to take AP or IB coursework and tests during your high school career. If you have high enough scores (often between 3 and 5 on an AP test and 6 or 7 on an IB test), you may be eligible for college credit or placement out of introductory-level courses. Contact your institution to learn more about its credit practices.

CLEP test: CLEP tests, which are less popular among high school students, are short exams covering a wide range of topics that can be used to earn college credit at some institutions. Check with your potential institutions to find out about their regulations and the minimum scores required for credit.

There is a lot to keep track of when applying to colleges.

Advanced Placement (AP) Courses and Dual Enrollment.

Advanced Placement (AP) classes and Dual Enrollment are two programs accessible to high school students to earn college credits before graduating.

Advanced Placement (AP) Courses: - **High Schools Offer:** AP classes are college-level courses taught in high school.

- **Standardised Curriculum:** Students pursue a standardised curriculum that culminates in an AP exam.

- AP Exams: Students can take an AP exam at the end of the course, and if they score well (typically a 3 or higher out of 5) they may receive college credit.

- **Rigorous Content:** AP courses are hard and demanding, designed to push students.

- **Wide Recognition:** They are widely recognised by colleges and institutions in the United States and around the world.

Dual Enrollment:
- Students can register in both high school and a local community college or university simultaneously.

- **Real College Courses:** Students take college-level courses that count towards both high school and college credits.

- **Flexible Schedule:** These classes can be offered during the high school day, in the evening, or online.

- **Transition to College:** This programme allows students to gain experience with genuine college homework and get a jump start on their studies.

- **It varies by institution:** Credit transfer policies can differ, so it's crucial to understand how these credits will be used to future college programmes.

Both alternatives are fantastic opportunities for determined individuals to advance, save money on college tuition, and push themselves academically. It is usually a good idea to check with school counsellors to see which option best fits a student's aspirations and college plans.

- Extracurricular Activities and Their Impact on College Admissions.

Extracurricular activities are activities that students engage in outside of their academic studies. Sports, clubs, charity work, music, art, and other activities are all options. They play an important part in college admissions. Here's why.

1. **Expresses your interests:** These activities allow you to demonstrate your interests outside of school. It informs colleges about your interests and activities.

2. **Demonstrates time management:** Being active outside of class demonstrates that

you can manage your time effectively, balancing schoolwork and other interests.

3.   **Develops   skills:**   Extracurricular activities can help you learn new abilities that aren't covered in class. This could include teamwork, leadership, and problem-solving.

4. ** Demonstrates commitment:** Colleges want to see that you are dedicated. Sticking with an activity for a long time demonstrates dedication.

5. **Gives a more complete picture of you:** Grades and exam scores do not reveal everything about you. Activities might help universities get a complete picture of who you are.

6. Networking: They allow you to meet new people and can lead to career contacts.

7. Leadership and Responsibility: If you hold a leadership position, it suggests that you possess leadership abilities and can handle responsibility.

8. **Contribution to campus life:** Colleges seek students who will contribute to campus life, and your extracurricular activities can demonstrate how you might do so.

9. **Diversity:** Your distinctive activities can enhance the diversity of a campus community.

10. **Could be a tiebreaker:** If you have equal grades and test scores as another applicant, your extracurricular activities may be what distinguishes you.

In conclusion, extracurricular activities are crucial in college admissions because they help schools learn more about who you are, what you are passionate about, and how you may contribute to their community. They demonstrate that you are not only concerned with academics, but also with your overall development. Remember, it's important to strike a balance; it's not just about doing a lot of things, but also about being truly interested in them.

College admissions tests (SAT, ACT, etc.).

College admission tests such as the SAT (Scholastic Assessment Test) and the ACT (American College Testing) are standardised exams taken by high school students in the United States when applying to colleges. Here's a quick summary of what they are and why they matter:

SAT:

 - **What it is:** The SAT assesses a student's college readiness and offers colleges with a standardised data point to compare applications.

- **Sections:** It has parts on math, reading, writing, and language.

- **Essay:** An optional essay was once available, but it has since been discontinued.

- **SCORING:** The Math and Evidence-Based Reading and Writing portions are graded on a 200-800 point scale, while the overall score spans from 400 to 1600.

- **Purpose:** Many institutions utilise SAT scores to choose which candidates to admission.

ACT:

- **What it is:** The ACT is another college entrance exam with a curriculum-based approach.

- **Sections**: It has four sections: English, Mathematics, Reading, and Science.

- **Writing Test:** There is an optional Writing Test (or essay).

- **SCORING:** The scores for each section range from 1 to 36. The composite score represents the average of the four components.
- **Purpose:** Like the SAT, colleges utilise ACT results to make admissions choices.

Common Points:

- **Test Prep:** Students frequently prepare for these exams by studying the material, taking practice tests, and learning test-taking skills.

- **Test Dates:** These tests are administered several times every year.

- **Register:** You must pre-register for the exams, and there is a charge, however waivers may be available for those in need.

- **University Consideration:** While some institutions are test-optional or test-blind, which means they do not require SAT or ACT scores, many continue to use these tests in the admissions process.

Both the SAT and ACT are designed to predict how well you will perform in college. A good score on these tests can occasionally compensate for poorer grades in high school, but more and more universities are considering the entire application—including grades, courses taken, essays, and extracurricular activities—when making their judgements. Always check the testing requirements for each college you're interested in, as they can differ!

Chapter 3:

College Research and Decision Making.

College research and decision-making are critical steps for students considering their higher education paths. It's about finding a college that meets your intellectual, personal, and economical requirements. Here's a quick guide on navigating this process.

Step One: Self-Assessment

Begin by identifying what you want and need from a college.

- **Interests and Goals:** Can you describe your academic interests? What career route do you plan to pursue?

- **Learning Style:** Do you prefer lectures, hands-on activities, or a combination?

- **Location Preference:** City, suburb, or rural? Closer to home or further away?

- **Size:** Do you envision yourself attending a huge institution or a small college?

- **Community:** What type of student body and campus culture do you envision?

Step 2: Research

Next, collect information about schools.

- **College Websites:** Learn about the programmes, professors, student life, and entrance requirements.

- At college fairs, meet representatives and ask questions.

- **Campus Visits:** If possible, visit colleges to gain a sense of the campus.

- **Online Forums and Reviews:** See what current students and graduates have to say about their experiences.

Step 3: Academic Programmes

Concentrate on what you want to study.

- **Majors and Minors:** Make sure your potential colleges provide the programme you're interested in.

- **Accreditation:** Determine whether the programmes are accredited by respectable agencies.

- **Faculty:** Look up professors in your preferred subject of study.

Step 4: Costs and Financial Aid

Figure out the financials:

- **Tuition and Fees:** Determine the total cost of attendance.

- **Financial Aid:** Investigate scholarships, grants, work-study, and loan opportunities.
- **ROI:** Consider the return on investment, or how much you might make after graduation.

Step 5: Admission Process

Know what's required to apply.

- **Deadlines:** Keep a record of all application deadlines.

- **Entrance Exams:** Prepare for any needed examinations, such as the SAT or ACT.

- **Application Materials:** Determine the essays, recommendation letters, and transcripts required.

Step 6: Create a Shortlist.

Narrow down your options:

- **Pros and Cons List:** Make a list that weighs each school's advantages and disadvantages.

- **Rank Preferences:** Rank colleges according to how well they meet your needs and desires.

Step 7: Final Decision

When making a final decision:

- **Revisit your research:** Review your notes and impressions.
- **Speak with Others:** Discuss your options with family, friends, mentors, or counsellors.

- **Listen to your gut:** Finally, evaluate where you felt most comfortable or optimistic about the future.

Step 8: Apply.

Once you've made your decision, apply to the colleges on your list.

- **Follow Instructions:** Ensure that all elements of the application are completed correctly.

- **Apply to a Range:** Specify safety, match, and reach schools.

- **Proofread:** Before submitting, thoroughly review all of your contents.

Step 9: Acceptance, and Beyond

After receiving your responses:

- **Evaluate Offers:** Consider the financial aid packages and overall prices.

- **Revisit as Needed:** If possible, return to the campuses of the universities that accepted you.

- **Decision Time** Make your final decision and notify the colleges.

Step ten: Prepare for college

Prepare for your college journey:

- **Housing:** Determine whether you will live in on-campus dormitories or off-campus housing.

- **Orientation:** Participate in any orientation programmes to become used to campus life.

- **Registration:** Register for classes as soon as you can.

Conclusion:

College research and decision-making can be time-consuming, but if you break it down into manageable phases and complete each one thoroughly, you'll be able to make a more informed and confident decision about your educational future.

Types of Colleges and Degrees (Community Colleges, Universities, Vocational Schools, Online Education.

Sure, let's put the many types of universities and degrees into simple terms:

Community colleges:

- **What They Are:** Community colleges are public educational institutions that provide two-year programmes leading to an Associate's degree. They are frequently utilised as a stepping stone to four-year universities.

- **Degrees Offered:** AA, AS, and AAS degrees. They also provide certificate programmes in certain vocations.

- **Key Features:** Reduced tuition, flexible scheduling, small class sizes, and vocational training programmes.

Universities:

- **What They Are:** Universities are major educational institutions that provide undergraduate, graduate, and postgraduate degrees. They frequently cover a wide range of academic subjects.

- **Degrees Available:** Bachelor's degrees (BA, BS), Master's degrees (MA, MS, MBA), Doctoral degrees (PhD, EdD, etc.), and professional degrees (JD, MD).

- **Key Features:** A diverse academic programme, research facilities, a variety of extracurricular activities, on-campus housing, and full-time faculty.

Vocational schools:

- **What They Are:** Also known as technical or trade schools, they offer hands-on instruction to prepare students for specialised trades or careers.

- **Degrees Offered:** Mostly diplomas or certificates for specific industries including welding, culinary arts, and medical assistance.

- **Key Features:** Career-specific curriculum, shorter programme lengths, and practical skills training that leads directly to employment.

Online education:

- **What They Are:** Online education allows students to learn from anywhere.

- **Degrees Offered:** Options include certificate programmes, associate's, bachelor's, master's, and doctoral degrees.

- **Key Features:** Flexible scheduling, accessibility (study from anywhere with an internet connection), and several self-paced courses.

In summary, community colleges are frequently local and less expensive stepping stones to higher education, universities offer a diverse range of undergraduate and graduate degrees in a variety of academic fields, vocational schools are ideal for those seeking specific, practical skillsets in short-term programmes, and online education provides flexibility and access without the need to attend a physical campus.

- Researching Colleges (using online tools and college fairs)

When it comes to investigating universities, you have a multitude of tools available both online and in person. Combining these tactics can help you gain a more comprehensive knowledge of which institutions may be a good fit for you. Here's a quick introduction to using online resources and attending college fairs to make informed judgements.

Online Tools

1. **College Websites** Begin by visiting the official websites of colleges that interest you. Look for details on programmes, teachers, campus life, and financial aid.
   - Investigate virtual campus tours, if available.

2. **Online College Databases and Search Tools** - Use platforms like the U.S. Department of Education's College Scorecard, College Board's BigFuture, and Peterson's to filter universities by location, size, majors, and other criteria.
   - Read up on graduation rates, average student debt, and other statistics.

3. **Social Media and Forums** - Follow colleges on Instagram, Twitter, and Facebook to learn about campus culture and latest news.
   - Check out student forums or platforms like Reddit to get honest feedback and answers from current or former students.

4. **Virtual College Fairs** - Participate in virtual college fairs to interact with admissions representatives, view webinars, and access resources. These activities are listed on websites such as NACAC (National Association for College Admission Counselling) or by individual colleges.

5. **Review and Ranking Sites** - Consider rankings and reviews from Niche or US News & World Report for extra data points, but keep in mind that they may not accurately reflect the student experience.

College Fairs.

1. **Preparation Before the Fair** - Determine when local or regional college fairs are held, typically in the fall or spring.
   - Before attending, develop a list of universities you're interested in that will be represented at the fair.

2. At the fair, question college representatives about admissions requirements, financial aid, student life, and programmes of interest.
   - Attend any available information sessions.
   - Gather pamphlets, business cards, and contact information for follow-up inquiries.

3. **After the Fair:** Organise the information you gathered.
  - Follow up with schools you're still interested in; send a thank you note and ask any more questions to the admissions reps you spoke with.

4. **Follow-Up Events** - Some college fairs provide follow-up events with longer presentations. If you're interested, mark these in your calendar.

Combining both approaches

- Compare the information you acquire from in-person interactions to what you obtain online. They should complement one another and assist you create a larger picture.
- Keep comprehensive notes, and perhaps a spreadsheet, noting the aspects of various universities that are essential to you.

- If possible, consider contacting current students or scheduling interviews with instructors in your subject of interest to obtain more personalised information.

Remember, the goal of college research is to locate a school where you can prosper academically, socially, and personally. Using both online tools and human contact at college fairs will provide you with a comprehensive view of your possibilities, allowing you to make the best decision for your future.

- Visiting Colleges (virtual tours if in-person visits aren't possible).

Visiting colleges is an exciting step on the path to higher education. It helps you to get a sense of the school, the students, and what the future may bring. However, distance, travel fees, or scheduling issues may prevent in-person visits. In such instances, virtual college visits can be a great option.

Virtual College Tours: A Simple Guide

1. Begin with the college website:
Most schools and universities provide virtual tours directly on their websites. These tools can be found by searching for "Virtual Tour," "Campus Visit," or "Prospective Students" links.

2: Use Search Engines:
Enter the college's name and the phrase "virtual tour" into a search engine. This can lead to virtual tours that are not immediately visible on the institution's official website, as well as third-party hosted experiences.

3. Social Media and YouTube: Many colleges share tour films on their social media pages or YouTube channels. These forums might offer a more informal perspective on college life.

4. Interactive Maps:

Interactive campus maps can sometimes provide a click-through experience for school highlights.

5. Virtual Reality (VR) Experiences:

Some colleges offer VR tours that provide a 360-degree perspective of campus. You may need a VR headset, but many can be seen with a smartphone or PC.

6. Virtual events:

Check out live virtual events including webinars, Q&A sessions with admissions professionals, and student panels. These typically allow you to ask inquiries in real time.

7. Contact us for more information:

If the virtual tour does not cover a region, please contact the admissions office via email or phone to request further information. They could have extra resources to offer.

Remember, whether in person or virtually, visiting a college is about seeing yourself there. Take notes on what you like and dislike, and ask lots of questions to ensure you locate the best fit for your educational journey.

- Applying to Colleges (application process, essays, letters of recommendation)

Applying to college can be a significant milestone in a student's life. The procedure includes numerous essential steps, each of which demands meticulous attention to detail. Here is a simple overview:

1. Research and Selection of Colleges:
   - Start by looking for institutions that offer the programmes you're interested in and fit your academic profile and personal preferences.

- Consider criteria such as location, size, school culture, and extracurricular activities.
- Make a balanced list of reach, match, and safety schools.

2. Understanding Application criteria: - Each college may have unique criteria. Standardised test scores (such as the SAT or ACT), high school transcripts, essays, interviews, and other materials may be requested.
- Check whether the colleges accept the Common Application, the Coalition Application, or their own system.

3. Preparing for standardised tests:
- If necessary, prepare for examinations such as the SAT or ACT by studying ahead of time and taking practice exams.
- Schedule your test dates ahead of time, and allow for retakes if necessary.

4. High school transcripts and grades:

- Continue your academics throughout high school, as your GPA is a crucial element of your college applications.

- Request that your official transcripts be delivered to the colleges you're applying to.

5. College Essays: - College essays allow you to showcase your personality beyond grades and test scores.

- Take the time to think and write appealing essays on your personality, experiences, and goals.

- Proofread your essays, and consider seeking comments from a teacher or mentor.

6. Letters of Recommendation: - Identify professors, counsellors, or mentors who can attest to your academic and personal strengths.

- Ask them well in advance of the application deadlines, and supply them with facts about yourself that will assist them in writing a detailed letter.

7. Filling Out the Application: - Provide accurate and detailed information in your application.Double-check every information to confirm it is correct.

- Complete any additional criteria specified by each college.

8. Application Fees and Waivers: - Most colleges need an application fee, however some may provide free applications.

- If the cost is onerous, look into fee waivers and see if you are eligible.

9. Submitting Your Application: - Check each college's deadlines, since some may provide early action or decision choices with earlier deadlines.

- Submit all components of your application by the deadline.

10. After Applying: - Some schools may request interviews, so be prepared to explain why you're interested in the programme and how you can contribute to the campus.

- Continue to concentrate on your high school studies; universities may want your last semester grades.

11. Financial Aid and Scholarships:

- Complete any eligible financial assistance forms, such as the Free Application for Federal Student assistance (FAFSA) and the CSS Profile.

- Apply for scholarships and grants provided by various organisations to help with educational expenses.

12. Waiting for Decision Letters: - After submitting your application, there will be a period of waiting until you receive admission decisions.

- Use this time to stay on top of your studies and learn about college accommodation, meal plans, and campus life.

13. Making Your Decision: - After receiving all acceptances, make your final decision. Consider all factors, including financial aid offers. Most colleges require decisions by May 1st.

14. Acceptance and Enrollment: After selecting a programme, you must accept the offer of admission and make any necessary deposits.
    - Follow the college's following actions to guarantee a smooth transition.

Remember that, while the process can be intimidating, remaining organised and starting early can make it easier to manage. Good luck!

- Financing College (scholarships, grants, loans, work-study programs).

Financing college may appear daunting, but there are various solutions available to assist manage the cost. Here's a quick summary of the major types:

1. **Scholarships**: - These money do not require repayment.
   - They can be given for a variety of reasons, including academic achievement, athletic ability, community service, and more.
   - Scholarships can come from a variety of sources, including schools, commercial businesses, and non-profit organisations.
   - To enhance your chances of obtaining rewards, start looking for scholarships early and apply to as many as you can.

2. **Grants**: Grants, like scholarships, are non-repayable.
   - They are frequently need-based, which means they are awarded depending on the student's or family's financial circumstances.
   - The Pell Grant is the most well-known federal grant, although other options include state and institutional grants.

3. **Loans**: - Borrowed money must be repaid with interest.

- Federal student loans often have lower interest rates and more flexible repayment choices than private loans.

- It is advisable to exhaust all federal loan alternatives before turning to private loans.

4. **Work-Study Programs**: Colleges provide part-time work opportunities as part of financial aid packages.

- Work-study positions are often on campus and may be related to your course of study or community service.

- Earned money can be used to pay for tuition, books, or other expenditures without having to be reimbursed.

To go across these options:

- Begin by completing the Free Application for Federal Student Aid (FAFSA) to determine what federal aid you are eligible for.

- Start looking for scholarships as early as your junior year in high school.

  - Research the grants available through your state or preferred college.
- If loans are required, review the terms and commit to a repayment plan that will work for you after graduation.
- If you are eligible for work study, take advantage of the opportunity to earn money while also gaining job experience.

Remember that a combination of these choices may be the best way to fund your college education.

Chapter 4:

Career Technical Education and Alternative Paths.

Career Technical Education (CTE) and alternative courses provide educational and professional opportunities that are distinct from the typical four-year college track. Here's a simplified view of each:

1. Career Technical Education (CTE):
- Concentrates on teaching specialised vocational skills.
- Provides hands-on training in a variety of sectors including healthcare, engineering, agriculture, and more.
- Can result in certifications or associate degrees.
- Apprenticeships allow you to learn on the job.
- Can be found at high schools, vocational schools, and community colleges.

2. **Alternative paths:**
These may include:
- Community college: A less expensive option for obtaining a two-year associate degree or transferring credits to a four-year university later.

- Trade schools are institutions that educate skills for specific trades such as welding, cosmetology, and culinary arts.

- Apprenticeships: Programmes in which you receive a wage while learning a skilled trade under the supervision of experienced workers.

- Online courses provide flexible learning opportunities that can lead to certifications or degrees.

- Military service: Offers employment training, educational perks, and a career path.

- Entrepreneurship: Starting your own business with a unique idea or skill set.

CTE and alternate paths allow individuals to obtain practical skills that can lead directly to employment or serve as a stepping stone to future study. These paths may be ideal possibilities for those who want to enter the workforce sooner, save on education expenditures, or want a more hands-on approach to learning.

- Trade Schools and Apprenticeships.

Trade schools and apprenticeships are two popular ways to learn a skilled trade through hands-on experience and study.

Trade Schools:

- Trade schools, often known as vocational schools or technical colleges, are postsecondary institutions that train students in specific trades.
- They give structured courses that combine classroom knowledge with practical skills applicable to occupations such as electricians, plumbers, cooks, and automotive specialists.
- Programmes at trade schools might last anywhere from a few months to two years.
- Students who complete trade school programmes typically receive certificates or diplomas, and in certain cases, associate degrees.

- Attending a trade school is usually less expensive and takes less time than getting a four-year college degree.
- The programme focuses on job-specific skills, allowing students to enter the field with a high degree of trade competency.

Apprenticeships:

- Apprenticeships involve both on-the-job training and, in many cases, classroom instruction.
- They take a hands-on approach, with apprentices hired and working under the supervision of experienced workers known as journeyworkers.
- Apprentices are paid while they study, and their income typically increases as they proceed through their training.
- Apprenticeships are prevalent in trades including carpentry, electrical work, plumbing, and machining, among others.
- Apprentices get substantial work experience and a thorough understanding of their craft at the

end of their apprenticeship, which can span anywhere from one to six years.
- Apprentices typically earn a nationally recognised credential or certification at the end of their training that demonstrates their proficiency in the trade.

Both trade schools and apprenticeships are efficient alternatives to learn the skills needed for many in-demand and well-paying jobs without requiring a standard four-year college degree. Both are geared towards people who love energetic, physical work and hands-on problem solving.

- Military Options

There are various paths you can take to develop a career in the military, and your options may differ based on your country and the branch of the military (Army, Navy, Air Force, Marines,

Coast Guard, etc.) you're interested in. Here are some generic options:

1. **Reserve Officers' Training Corps (ROTC)**: In the United States, several colleges and institutions offer ROTC programmes, which combine military training with ordinary academic courses. Students can obtain scholarships that cover tuition and fees in exchange for pledging to serve in the military following graduation. Other countries might have comparable programmes.

2. **Service Academies**: In the United States, these schools include the United States Military Academy (West Point), the Naval Academy, the Air Force Academy, and the Coast Guard Academy. These are extremely competitive, providing a tough academic and military education. Graduates are commissioned officers upon completion. Other nations have their own versions of military academies.

3. **Direct Commission**: Some professions, such as medicine, law, or chaplaincy, may provide direct commissioning opportunities. This course is for those who have completed their civilian education and desire to join the military as officers.

4. **Enlisted-to-Officer Programmes**: If you enter the military as an enlisted member, you can often participate in programmes that will assist you become an officer, such as Officer Candidate School (OCS) or Officer Training School (OTS).

5. **Civilian Colleges and Universities**: While attending a civilian college or university, you can pursue degrees that are useful in the military, such as engineering, computer science, international relations, or other disciplines that the military values.

6. **Vocational and Technical Training**: Military-friendly vocational institutions can help you prepare for military professions in a variety of technical fields, including mechanics and information technology specialists.

7. **Junior Reserve Officers' Training Corps (JROTC)**: High schools may provide JROTC programmes to expose pupils to military skills and leadership training.

8. **Specialised Military Schools**: Depending on your interests, you may want to pursue specialised military education in areas such as cybersecurity, intelligence, or engineering.

To prepare for a military career, it is important to establish a strong physical fitness routine, leadership qualities, and a solid understanding of military history and culture. It is also critical to research the exact admission requirements and expectations for the country and branch of service you intend to join. Remember that the path to a military profession can be highly hard, requiring a dedication not just to the educational process but also to service commitments after graduation.

- Gap Year Opportunities

A gap year is a year off between graduating from high school and attending college. So, rather than starting college the fall after you graduate from high school, you'd start the following fall.

Gap years are intended to provide students a respite from studies. It's usually a time to discover oneself and decide what kind of education and career path you want to pursue.

A gap year can take various shapes. For example, you could work, do an internship, volunteer, or travel. These activities can be completed alone or as part of a gap year programme.

Taking a gap year can provide an excellent opportunity for personal development, adventure, and learning outside of regular academic settings. Here's a quick guide to some of the options accessible during a gap year:

1. Volunteer Work • **Local Opportunities**: Begin by volunteering at local shelters, food banks, and non-profit organisations.
- **Abroad Programmes**: Work with overseas organisations to promote causes such as wildlife conservation, community development, and education.

2. Internships - **Professional Fields**: Gain experience and network in desired fields through internships in firms, NGOs, or government entities.
- **Startup Experience**: Collaborate with a startup in a dynamic learning environment where you can wear multiple jobs.

3. Travel - **Backpacking**: A budget-friendly way to explore cultures, languages, and landscapes across countries.

- **Cultural Immersion**: Spend enough time in one region to fully immerse oneself in the language and culture.

4. Education - **Language Learning**: Enrol in language schools overseas to master a new language.
- **Skill Courses**: Take lessons in computing, scuba diving, or culinary skills.

5. Work Abroad - **Au Pair**: Live with a host family in another country to help with childcare and light housework.
- **Teaching English**: Become certified to teach English as a foreign language and work in schools all around the world.

6. Adventure and Exploration - **Outdoor Programmes**: Participate in outdoor adventure programmes such as hiking, kayaking, or rock climbing.

- **Conservation Projects**: Work in national parks or animal reserves to help protect the environment.

7. Personal Projects - **Creative Pursuits**: Spend time on writing, art, music, or other creative activities.
- **Entrepreneurship: Create your own project or business by researching, planning, and executing a concept that you are enthusiastic about.

8. Academic Enrichment - **Research Projects**: Participate in or lead a research project related to your interests.
- **Pre-college Programmes**: Take courses at universities that provide summer sessions for high school students or those taking a gap year.

9. Specialist Programs - **Marine Programmes**: Collaborate with conservation organisations, learn to dive, and research marine biology.

- **Technology Bootcamps**: Attend tech boot camps to learn to code or improve your IT skills.

10. Combination Programs - **Structured Gap Year Programmes**: Join programmes that combine travel, volunteering, and education for gap year students.

Plan Your Gap Year - **Begin Early**: Start preparing your gap year months in advance to investigate options and acquire placements or funds.

- **Budget**: Create a budget to manage your spending, taking into account any necessary travel insurance, vaccines, and visas.

- **Set goals**: Determine your goals—whether it's learning a new skill, acquiring work experience, or simply experiencing the world.

- **Remain flexible**: Be flexible and adapt your plans as opportunities occur.

Remember, a gap year allows you to get out of your comfort zone, challenge yourself, and grow in unexpected ways. Investigate your alternatives, plan thoroughly, but leave room for spontaneity and adventure.

- Direct-to-Workforce Prospects.

"Direct-to-Workforce Prospects" refers to chances that allow people to enter the workforce directly, frequently without the traditional four-year college degree. Here's a simple explanation:

Direct-to-workforce prospects are avenues that allow people to begin working and earning money right immediately. They're great for people who wish to skip the lengthy and expensive schooling process and get immediately into a career. Here are a few ways to accomplish this:

1. **Vocational Training:** Short-term courses that teach specific job skills such as welding, plumbing, and electrical work.

2. **Apprenticeships:** Combining on-the-job training with some classroom study, apprenticeships allow you to learn a skill while working and frequently lead to employment.

3. **Certification Programmes:** These programmes provide specialised training in industries such as information technology, healthcare, and hospitality, and can take anywhere from a few months to a year to finish.

4. **On-the-Job Training**: Some companies train employees on the job. You begin working and learn as you go, for cash.

5. *Military Service:** Joining the military can be a straight path to employment, with training available in a variety of sectors.

6. Entrepreneurship:** Starting a small business can allow you to work for yourself right away, but it is typically dangerous and needs a significant amount of effort.

These possibilities may lead to solid work opportunities and a steady income without requiring years of formal education. Furthermore, they are frequently in demand and cannot be readily outsourced or automated.

**Chapter 5:

Soft Skills and Personal Development**.

Soft skills are personal characteristics that influence how effectively you connect with others. These abilities help you improve your relationships, job performance, and career chances. Soft skills, as opposed to technical or "hard" skills, are concerned with how you do specific activities, such as communication, teamwork, and problem-solving.

Personal development activities include improving self-awareness and identity, developing abilities and potential, increasing human capital, and facilitating employability. Personal development is the quest of improving one's quality of life and realising one's dreams and aspirations.

Simply put, soft skills are interpersonal abilities that allow you to navigate your environment, collaborate well with people, perform successfully, and achieve your goals while complementing your hard skills. Personal development is the process of improving yourself and controlling your personal and professional growth.

- Communication skills.

Communication skills are extremely crucial in our daily lives. They are the instruments we use to express our thoughts, ideas, and emotions to others. Here are some basic fundamental points about communication abilities.

1. **Listening**: One important aspect of communication is listening to others. When you listen properly, you grasp what the other person is saying, which demonstrates your concern.

2. **Speaking**: Speaking clearly allows people to comprehend you. It is not only important to choose the right words, but also to express them correctly. Speak at a comfortable speed and with clarity.

3. **Body Language**: Our bodies also communicate! Your facial expressions, hand gestures, and posture all convey clues about how you feel and think.

4. **Eye Contact**: Looking someone in the eyes demonstrates confidence and helps create trust.

5. **Being Clear and Concise**: Say what you mean without using excessive words. This makes the message simpler and easier to understand.

6. **Empathy**: Try to comprehend other people's emotions and see things through their eyes. This enables you to communicate in a caring manner.

7. **Asking Questions**: If you're unsure about something, ask questions. It demonstrates your attention while also reducing confusion.

8. **Feedback**: Providing and receiving feedback is an effective strategy to improve communication. Just make sure to do it in a kind, productive manner.

9. **Adapting**: Because everyone is different, you may need to communicate differently with each person. Paying attention to how they react can help you determine whether you need to change your manner.

10. **Staying cheerful**: Even when addressing difficult things, strive to remain cheerful. It makes communication easier and more pleasant.

Remember that you can always improve your communication skills. It's similar to playing a sport or an instrument: the more you practise, the better you get!

- Time Management.

Time management is all about organising and arranging how much time you spend on various tasks. It's crucial because it allows you to work smarter, not harder, so you can get more done in less time, even when time is limited and pressures are high. Here's a simple way to organise your time:

1. **Set Goals**: Determine what you want to accomplish in one day, a week, or a month. Make sure your goals are SMART (Specific, Measurable, Achievable, Relevant, and Time-bound).

- S—Clearly state your goal.
- M—Ensure you can measure your goal.
- A—Set goals you know you can achieve.

- R—Set goals relevant to your career or education.
- T—Set a deadline for completion.

2. **Prioritise**: Not everything that can be done has to be completed. Determine which chores are the most vital and require your immediate attention. Do them first.

3. **Create A To-Do List**: At the outset of each day, jot down the chores that must be performed. It's satisfying to mark off items as they're accomplished!

4. **Prepare Ahead**: Use calendars and planners. To avoid last-minute rush, plan ahead of time by a week or a month.

5. **Limit Distractions**: Put away or turn off anything that could disrupt your concentration, such as your phone or television.

6. **Set Time Limits**: Setting a time limit for an activity will help you avoid spending too much time on one item. Set timers as necessary.

7. **Take Breaks**: Our minds can only concentrate for so long before needing to rest. Short, frequent breaks can help you maintain a steady level of productivity.

8. **Learn to Say No**: If you are too busy to take on more, it is acceptable to decline more duties or requests for your time.

9. **Review the Time Spent**: At the end of the week, reflect on your efforts and identify areas for improvement.

By effectively organising your time, you will have more time to devote to both enjoyable activities and necessary chores.

- Teamwork and Leadership.

Teamwork and leadership are two sides of the same coin, both critical to the success of any group or organisation. Each plays a unique role but shares a common goal: to achieve a collective outcome that is greater than the sum of individual efforts.

Teamwork

Teamwork is the joint effort of a group of people working towards a common goal. It is based on varied individuals contributing their unique skills, experiences, and viewpoints to solve issues or achieve goals. Effective teamwork can result in new ideas that would not have been achievable with individual effort alone.

The Characteristics of Good Teamwork

- **Communication:** Team members must speak openly and honestly in order to share ideas, provide feedback, and raise issues.

- **Collaboration:** Collaboration entails working together to complete tasks in an efficient and productive manner.

- **Trust:** Teamwork thrives when members believe in each other's abilities and intentions.

- **Flexibility:** Teams must frequently adjust to new information, difficulties, or organisational changes.

- **Commitment:** Every team member must be dedicated to the group effort and driven to do their best work.

- **Diversity:** A diverse set of talents, backgrounds, and viewpoints can improve teamwork and lead to greater results.

- **Conflict Resolution:** Addressing and managing conflict constructively is a necessary component of effective teamwork.

Leadership.

Setting the group's direction, motivating members, and providing an engaging and inspiring environment are all aspects of leadership. A successful leader not only manages and directs, but also helps to develop the team's full potential, allowing each member to contribute effectively to the shared goals.

The Qualities of Effective Leadership:

- **Vision:** Leaders must create a clear and compelling vision that will guide the team's activities.

- **Empathy:** Understanding each team member's point of view and creating a supportive environment is critical.

- **Decisiveness:** Leaders must make judgements quickly and confidently, even when under pressure.

- **Integrity:** Trust in leadership is based on consistency, honesty, and ethical behaviour.

- **Influence:** Effective leaders encourage others to follow them and work towards the team's goals.

- **Inclusivity:** A leader should create an environment in which all team members feel appreciated and may grow.

Interplay of Teamwork and Leadership

Leadership and teamwork are linked. A good leader is required to effectively guide a team, and a cohesive team is necessary for a leader to realise a vision. Leaders arise from teams, which require leaders for coordination and purpose.

How they work together:

- A leader articulates the vision and guides the team's efforts to achieve it.
- Teams provide input to leaders, allowing for changes to strategy and tactics.
- Leaders promote teamwork by fostering a collaborative environment and resolving challenges that hamper development.
- Teams provide leaders with the support and on-the-ground knowledge required for sound decision-making.

151

- A synergy between leader and team frequently develops in shared leadership, in which different members take the lead on tasks that are relevant to their expertise.

Conclusion:

The balance between cooperation and leadership is critical to the success of any business. Leaders must be skilled at encouraging teamwork, and teams must be willing to follow and be influenced by their leaders. An environment that values mutual respect, shared responsibility, and collaborative effort will improve the effectiveness of both elements, resulting in the organization's success and growth.

- Problem Solving and Critical Thinking.

Okay, let's reduce these two crucial concepts:

Problem Solving:

Imagine you have a large puzzle with many components. Problem solving is similar to putting this puzzle together. It entails looking at a challenging situation and determining how to resolve it. It is about thinking up new methods to improve something or discover a solution to a problem.

Here are the steps you could take to address a problem.

1. **Understand the Problem**: First and foremost, you must understand the issue at hand.

Look at the puzzle pieces to see what picture you need to create.

2. **Plan**: Consider how you can fix the situation. It's similar to solving a problem by starting with the corners.
3. **Try Solutions**: Begin assembling the components according to your idea. If one component doesn't fit, try another.

Critical Thought:

Now, critical thinking is similar to being a detective with that riddle. It's not just about finding pieces that fit, but also about understanding why they fit and whether there's a better place for them to go.

It includes a few crucial things:

1. **Questioning**: Don't simply accept things as they are. Ask questions such as "Why is this

piece important?" or "What happens if I put this here?".

2. **Analysing**: Examine all of the components you have carefully. Understand how they function both independently and in conjunction with other parts.

3. **Evaluating**: Determine whether the components make sense where they are or if anything needs to be moved. It's about making sound decisions.

4. **Reflecting**: Once you've begun to solve the challenge, take a step back and consider the process. Are things going well? What could be better?

Both problem solving and critical thinking are useful in everyday situations. They're like tools in your toolbox that you can use when you're unsure what to do, whether it's repairing a bike, determining what to buy, or solving a maths problem. They assist you in making informed

155

decisions and obtaining the information you require.

- Networking and Building Professional Relationships.

Networking and developing professional ties are similar to planting a garden. It's all about planting seeds, nurturing plants, and eventually reaping fruits that benefit everyone involved. Let us break it down into simple steps.

Planting Seeds: Initial Contacts

1. **Introduce Yourself**: Begin by meeting others. This could occur at work, at events, or even online via professional social media networks such as LinkedIn.

2. **Be Curious**: Inquire about what others do. Show genuine interest in their work and background.

3. **Common Ground**: Find shared hobbies or experiences to begin connecting.

Nurturing Relationships: Building Connections

1. **Follow-Up**: After the meeting, send a message noting how nice it was to meet them. This might be an email, a message on LinkedIn, or even a handwritten note, if appropriate.

2. **Share Resources**: If you come across an article or resource that could be useful to someone you've met, share it with them. It shows that you are considering their needs and interests.

3. **Support Others**: Celebrate their successes, offer assistance when they face challenges, and maintain a positive attitude.

157

Growing Together: Strengthening Bonds

1. **Consistency**: Keep in touch on a regular basis, not just when you need something. It can be as simple as catching up over coffee or chatting briefly on social media.

2. **Collaborate**: Seek for opportunities to work on projects together or introduce them to people who can help them grow.

3. **Trust**: Your actions should demonstrate that you are reliable and trustworthy. This includes meeting deadlines, keeping promises, and remaining discreet if they provide confidential information.

Enjoying The Harvest: The Advantages Of A Strong Network

1. **Opportunities**: As you establish a good reputation, you will likely receive new job opportunities, resources, and ideas.

2. **Support**: During difficult times, your network can provide advice, referrals, and a sympathetic ear.

3. **Friendship**: Professional relationships can evolve into personal friendships, bringing joy and fulfilment outside of work.

Keep The Garden Thriving: Continuous Networking

1. **Update Contacts**: If you change employment or receive a promotion, notify your network. They will enjoy being kept in the loop.

2. **Expand**: Always look for new people to join your network. Fresh contacts provide new perspectives and opportunities.

3. **Give Back**: As you achieve success, seek for ways to help others advance in their jobs.

To summarise, networking is the process of building a professional community around you. This community not only enhances your career, but also enriches it with knowledge, experience, and support. Remember that every connection counts, and a little compassion and curiosity can help you develop long-term professional relationships.

**Chapter 6:

Boss Battle - Dealing with Bullies*

Introduction:

Throughout our lives, we may face daunting challenges that test our courage and resolve. Consider these moments to be "boss battles," pivotal points in which we face obstacles that appear larger than life. Dealing with bullies is one of the most difficult challenges. No hero's journey is without adversaries, and bullies, with their intimidating demeanour and perplexing behaviour, can appear to be formidable bosses.

But don't worry; this chapter will help you navigate the treacherous waters of bullying. We will provide you with the knowledge to understand the nature of bullying, recognise the signs, and, most importantly, strategies to confront bullies with confidence and resilience. Just as a boss battle tests a video game character's skill and wit, confronting a bully provides an opportunity to grow stronger, wiser, and more compassionate.

So, take a deep breath and prepare for this crucial boss battle. Turning the page not only advances the story, but also marks the first step towards mastering the art of dealing with bullies. Together, we will learn how to turn a difficult battle into a spiritual victory. Welcome to your boss battle; let's win with dignity and grace.

- Identifying the Enemy: Recognizing Different Forms of Bullying.

Identifying the various forms of bullying is critical for recognising and addressing the problem in any setting, whether at school, work, or online. Bullying is more than just physical aggression; it takes many forms, each with its own set of characteristics and consequences. Here's a straightforward breakdown of the various types of bullying

1. **Definition: **Physical Bullying**** This is the most visible form of bullying, and it involves causing physical pain or harm to the victim. It includes hitting, kicking, pinching, tripping, and other forms of physical assault.

- *Signs:* Bruises, scratches, torn clothing, or multiple unexplained injuries.

2. Definition of Verbal Bullying. It encompasses name-calling, insults, teasing, intimidation, homophobic or racist remarks, and verbal abuse.

- *Signs:* The victim may exhibit symptoms of emotional distress, such as being unusually withdrawn, anxious, or having a drop in self-esteem.

3. Define "Social or Relational Bullying": Social bullying is more subtle than physical bullying and aims to harm someone's reputation or social standing.

. It may include spreading rumours, encouraging others to exclude someone, or publicly embarrassing them.

- *Signs:* The individual may become isolated, change their usual circle of friends, or exhibit changes in their social behaviours.

4. Definition of Cyberbullying This type of bullying occurs through digital devices such as cell phones, computers, and tablets. It includes sending, posting, or sharing negative, harmful, false, or derogatory content about others.

  - *Signs:* Reluctance to use a computer or mobile device, anxiety when receiving an alert, an unexpected drop in online activity, or abrupt mood changes after using the internet or texting.

5. **Psychological Bullying:** (Definition:) This is about inflicting psychological harm on someone. It is the manipulation and undermining of a person's confidence and sense of well-being.

  - *Signs:* The victim may appear unusually sensitive, sullen, or experience severe mood swings. They may also avoid situations in which they will come into contact with the bully.

6. Definition of Sexual Bullying. This includes harmful, humiliating, or coercive sexual behaviour. It can range from offensive remarks to unwanted touching or sexual assault.

- *Signs:* Withdrawal from social interaction, unexplained behavioural changes, or reluctance to visit locations where the bully may be present.

7. **Property Damage Bullying:** - *Definition:* This type of bullying involves targeting someone's possessions by stealing, breaking, or vandalising them.
- *Signs:* Personal items are missing or damaged, with no reasonable explanation.

To effectively combat bullying, it is critical to recognise its various forms and understand that a person may face more than one type of bullying. If you notice these symptoms in yourself or someone else, you must take action. Speak with a trusted friend, teacher, family member, or counsellor, and remember that you are not alone, and bullying is not tolerated in any form.

- Winning Strategies: Effective Ways to Stand Up to Bullies.

Yes, standing up to bullies can be delicate, but there are effective strategies that can be used to do so with confidence and adaptability. It's essential to keep effects simple and straightforward. Then are several strategies explained in a simple way

1. ** Remain Calm and Confident **- ** Calmness ** Keep your cool. Bullies frequently seek a response, so remaining calm takes down their power. - ** Confidence ** Maintain a establishment posture and speak easily. You don't have to be aggressive, but displaying confidence can discourage a bully.

2. ** Use Assertive Communication **- ** Speak easily ** Say what you have to say

easily. Use expressions similar as" I do not like what you are doing" or" Please stop that." - ** The Direct Language ** Avoid being nebulous. Be direct and regardful. For illustration," I want you to stop calling me names."

**3. ** Avoid Escalation **- ** Walk Down ** If a situation escalates, it's stylish to leave. This is not poltroonery; it's prudent to avoid a worse situation. - ** Change the Subject ** To lessen any pressure, try changing the subject or diverting the discussion.

**4. ** Stick With musketeers **- ** Safety in figures ** Bullies are less likely to target those who are with musketeers. - ** Support System ** musketeers can offer emotional support and may indeed defend you if a bully approaches.

**5. Practice tone- Defense- ** Learn Chops ** Understanding   tone- defense can boost confidence. This isn't to say you should fight, but it's about feeling safe. - ** Physical Posture

** Displaying a sense of physical security can discourage implicit bullies.

**6. ** Report Bullying **- ** Tell Someone ** communicate a schoolteacher, parent, or superior. It isn't dishing; it's taking action to help commodity bad from passing. • ** Document Incidents ** Keep track of bullying incidents so that you can report it if necessary.

7. Develop managing strategies, including relaxation ways like deep breathing and contemplation, to manage stress. ** Positive tone- Talk ** Remind yourself of your worth, and do not let a bully's words impact how you perceive yourself.

**8. ** Be visionary **- ** Education ** Learn about bullying and why it occurs. This can help you realise it's not your fault. - ** help others ** If you notice someone differently being bullied, stand up for them(safely) or seek backing.

**9. ** Avoid Bully Alarms **- ** Safe Routes ** Consider taking different paths to avoid the bully. - ** Understand Patterns ** Knowing when and where bullying occurs allows you to be more set or avoid certain situations.

**10. ** Seek Professional Help **- ** Counselling ** A counsellor can offer acclimatized strategies to help you make adaptability. - ** Support Groups ** Joining a support group can help you realise you aren't alone and that others have successfully overcome bullying.

Flash back, the thing isn't to fight or come a bully yourself, but to demonstrate that you value yourself and won't be an easy target. It's about asserting your rights without violating the rights of others. Each situation is unique, so it's critical to assess the environment and use your judgement to elect the stylish strategy.

- Summoning Help: When and How to Get Adults Involved.

Dealing with bullying can be challenging, perplexing, and frightening. As a teen, you may not always know when it's appropriate to involve an adult. Here's a simple guide to determining when and how to seek help.

When to Summon Help:

1. **Physical harm:** - If someone physically harms you in any way, you must notify an adult right away. Physical safety is the top priority.

2. Report any threats made against you, your possessions, or someone you care about.

3. **Emotional Harm:** - If bullying includes name-calling, intimidation, or causes you to feel unsafe or upset over time, seek help right away.

4. **Cyberbullying:** - Online bullying can be continuous. If you are being harassed, threatened, or bullied on social media or via text, it is time to seek help.

5. **Property Damage:** - If your belongings are stolen, damaged, or tampered with, please notify an adult.

** Repeated Incidents ** – While individual incidents may feel minor, a pattern of bullying geste
            is a serious problem that requires professional intervention.

7. **Escalation:** - If the bullying worsens or you experience increased anxiety or fear, seek help right away.

8. **Peer Inaction:** - If those around you are bullying you or failing to prevent it, seek adult help.

9. **Impact on Well-Being:** - If your mental health, schoolwork, or attendance are suffering, it's time for adult help.

10. **Gut Feeling:** Follow your instincts. If something feels wrong and you're struggling, speak with someone.

How to summon help:

1. Select a trustworthy adult to help, such as a parent, teacher, school counsellor, or coach.

2. **Be Direct:** - Emphasise that you need to discuss a serious matter. Use simple language, such as "I'm being bullied and need help."

3. **Explain the Situation:** - Explain exactly what happened, when it happened, who was involved, and how it affected you. The more information you can provide, the more likely the adult will understand and assist.

4. **Express Your Feelings:** - Tell the adult how you feel about the situation. Adults are not always aware of the emotional consequences of bullying.

5. **Ask for Specific Help:** - Tell the adult what assistance you need. Do you want them to intervene directly, help you speak with authorities, or simply listen and offer advice?

6. **Follow Up:** - If the initial conversation does not result in a change, do not give up. Speak up again, or find another adult who is willing to take action.

Remember, you don't have to deal with bullying alone. It is critical to involve adults who can help put an end to the situation and guide you through the procedure. You should feel protected and respected.

Chapter 7:

The Application Process (Jobs and Colleges)**

While the application processes for employment and universities are different, they do have certain similarities, such as preparation, submission of required papers, and a succession of subsequent procedures. Here's a quick summary of each:

Job Application Procedure:

1. **Research**: Begin by learning about possible employers' beliefs, culture, and the requirements for open positions.

2. **Resume/CV Preparation**: Tailor your resume or CV to showcase your most relevant experience, abilities, and accomplishments for the position you're applying for.

3. **Cover Letter**: Write a cover letter that explains how your abilities and experiences match the job requirements and the company's aims.

4. **Application Submission**: Submit your application using the employer's preferred method, which may be an internet portal, email, or physical mail.

5. **Follow-Up**: After submitting your application, you may want to follow up to check that it was received and to reiterate your interest in the position.

6. **Interview**: If selected, prepare for the interview by researching common questions, practicing responses, and being prepared to share your background in depth.

7. **Assessment**: Some employers may demand assessments or tests to determine your abilities.

8. **Reference Check**: Provide professional references as needed.

9. **Job Offer**: If you are successful, the employer will give you a job offer that you may accept, negotiate, or decline.

10. **Onboarding**: Once accepted, you will go through the onboarding process, which includes documentation, orientation, and training.

179

College Application Procedure:

1. **Research**: Look at colleges and universities to see what programmes, campus culture, and other offerings are compatible with your academic and personal goals.

2. **Standardised examinations**: Many institutions demand scores on standardised examinations like the SAT or ACT. Prepare and schedule these examinations well in advance.

3. **Application Forms**: Complete application forms, which are frequently available via online platforms such as the Common Application, which many colleges accept.

4. **Personal Statement/Essay**: Create a personal statement or essay explaining your background, experiences, and motivation for pursuing further education.

5. **Transcripts**: Request that your official high school transcripts be delivered to the universities you're applying to.

6. **Letters of Recommendation**: Request letters of recommendation from instructors, counsellors, or mentors who can attest to your abilities and character.

7. **Portfolios/Auditions**: Some programmes, such as the arts, may require you to submit a portfolio of your work or perform an audition.

8. **Interviews**: Some institutions may demand or provide optional interviews as part of the application process.

9. **Financial Aid**: Fill out financial aid applications, such as the FAFSA or the CSS Profile for institutional aid.

10. **Application analyse**: After submission, the admissions committee will analyse your application and make a judgement on admission.

181

11. **Decision**: The college will notify you whether you have been accepted, denied, or placed on the waitlist.

12. **Enrollment**: If approved, you may need to attend an orientation, select lodging, and enrol in classes.

Meeting application deadlines is crucial in both stages, and staying organised can assist ensure a seamless application experience.

- Writing Resumes and Cover Letters.

Writing resumes and cover letters is an important skill for job hunting. Both documents act as your personal marketing assets for potential employers. I'll divide the procedure into clear, actionable steps.

Writing a Resume

A resume is a brief document that summarises your education, work experience, abilities, and accomplishments relevant to the position you're looking for.

Format & Layout

1. Select a clear, professional typeface, such as Arial or Times New Roman.
2. **Keep the layout clean**, and use bold and italics sparingly to emphasise vital material.

3. Depending on your experience, try to keep it to one or two pages.

Resume Sections

: 1. **Contact Information**: - Include your name, phone number, email address, and optional LinkedIn profile.
    - Make sure your email is professional.

2. **Objective or Summary** (optional): - Briefly describe your career goals or skills and achievements.

3. **Education**: - Include your most current or relevant education first.
   - Include your degree, institution, graduation date, and any honours.

4. **Work Experience**: Arrange your jobs in reverse chronological order.
   - Include the work title, firm name, dates of employment, and bullet points summarising major responsibilities and accomplishments.

5. **Skills**: - Include both hard skills (such as software proficiency) and soft skills (e.g. communication).

6. **Certifications & Awards** (where applicable):
   - All relevant qualifications, licences, and awards.

7. **Volunteer Work and Projects** (optional):
   - Any unpaid efforts or projects that demonstrate relevant abilities or expertise.

Content Tip:

 Use Action Words Begin bullet points with verbs such as managed, developed, etc.
- **Quantify Your Achievements**: To demonstrate impact, use numbers (for example, "increased sales by 20%").

- **Customise Your Information** to match the job description, emphasising the most relevant experience.

Writing a Cover Letter

A cover letter is a one-page document that describes why you are the best applicant for the position.

Format & Layout

1. **Match the resume design** for uniformity.

2. **Select a simple, professional font**.

3. **Keep it to three or four paragraphs** and under one page.

Cover Letter Sections

1. **Contact Information**: - Include your name, phone number, and email address at the top of the letter, followed by the date and employer information.

2. **Salutation**: - Address the recruiting manager by name, e.g., "Dear Mr. Smith".

3. **Opening Paragraph**: - Introduce the job you're looking for and explain why you're interested.

4. **Body Paragraph(s)**: - Explain why you are a good fit with specific examples. Tell a tale

or explain a project that demonstrates your skills in action.

5. **Closing Paragraph**: Summarise why you are a good fit.
    - Clearly express what action you intend to take next, such as an interview.
    - I appreciate the reader's time and thoughtfulness.

6. **Formal Closing**: - End with "Sincerely," "Best regards," or a comparable professional sign-off.

Tips for Content.

- **Tailor Each Letter**: Customise your cover letter for each application to demonstrate your knowledge of the organisation and position.

- **Highlight Your Personal Value**: Make your case for what you bring to the table and how it applies to the job.

- **Use a Positive Tone**: Be confident and optimistic in your writing.

- **Proofreading**: Always check for spelling and grammar issues.

Remember that your resume presents the facts, but your cover letter tells the story of why those facts matter. Both documents should be polished, professional, and tailored to the position and firm you're applying for.

- Filling Out Applications.

Filling out applications, whether for a job, a loan, a rental property, or educational purposes, requires providing information about oneself in a clear, concise, and truthful manner. Here's a quick guide on how to fill out applications effectively:

Step 1: Gather Needed Information

Before you begin, make sure you have all of the information you'll probably need, including:

- Personal information (full name, address, phone number, email address).

- Social Security number (if applicable).

- Work experience (company names, positions, dates of work)

- Educational background (institutional names, degrees, and dates of attendance)

- References (names, relationships, contact details)

- Professional licences or certifications (where relevant)

Step 2: Read the instructions carefully.

Each application is unique, so read the directions carefully to understand what information is necessary and how it should be presented.

Step 3: Provide Personal Details

Fill in your name, address, contact information, and any other personal information precisely as requested. Ensure there are no typos or errors.

Step 4: Employment and Education History

Provide your relevant professional experience and educational background. Start with the most recent experience and work backwards. Be precise with your dates and include specifics about your tasks and accomplishments.

Step 5: Answer the Application Questions

Some applications may include explicit questions about the position or aim of the application. Answer these questions thoroughly and deliberately, while remaining honest and relevant.

Step 6: Provide References If necessary, list references with their consent and current contact information.

Step 7: Review your inputs

After you've finished filling out all of the forms, carefully evaluate your application for errors or missing information. Spell-check your work and ensure that all of your facts are right.

Step 8: Attach the necessary documents.

If the application requires extra papers (such as a resume, cover letter, or transcripts), include them as asked. Make sure they are properly formatted and relevant to the application.

Step 9: Submit your application

Follow the guidelines for submitting your application. This could include pressing the'submit' button for online applications, sending an email, or delivering a physical copy.

Step 10: Follow-up

In the event of job applications or other applications that require follow-up, make a note of when you filed your application and prepare to follow up if you have not heard back within the required time period.

Additional Tips:

- **Be Neat**: When filling out physical forms, use a black or blue pen to write legibly.

- **Be Honest**: It is critical that the information you offer is true.

- **Stay related**: Only include information related to the application.

- .- **Proofread**: Look for typos and grammar errors.

- **Keep Copies**: Save a copy of the completed application for your records.

Filling out applications can be a simple chore if you approach it step by step and keep organised. Always take the time to make sure your application represents you in the best possible light.

- Interview Techniques and Practice.

Sure, let's break down interview strategies and practice into simple steps:

1. Research - **Company Knowledge:** Gain insight into the company's culture, mission, news, and industry developments. Use their website, social media, and current press releases to do this.

- **Role Clarification:** Ensure that you understand the job description and how your talents fit the needs. Consider how you've used these skills in the past.

2. Self-Reflection - **Strengths and Weaknesses:** Identify your own abilities and places for improvement. Prepare to debate these frankly, with examples.

- **Professional Experience:** Have clear, concise tales about your previous work experiences, particularly those that are relevant to the position you are applying for.

3. Common Questions Prepare answers:** Common questions are "Tell me about yourself," and "Why do you want this job?" with the question "What's a challenge you've faced and how did you overcome it?" Have the answers ready.

- **Behavioural Question:** To structure responses to behavioural questions, use the STAR technique (Situation, Task, Action, and Results).

4. Mock interviews**Simulate the interview with a friend or family member. It will make you more comfortable talking about your experiences.

- **Record yourself:** If feasible, record your responses and replay them to identify where you can improve in terms of clarity and presentation.

5. Question Preparation Prepare your questions:** You should also prepare questions for the interviewer about the team, corporate culture, and expectations.

6. Dress Code: **Professional Attire**. Dress appropriately for the industry; when in doubt, lean towards formality. Make sure your dress is clean and well-fitted.

7. Non-Verbal Communication - **Body Language:** Use good posture, keep eye contact, and moderate gestures to explain oneself.

- **Listening Skills:** Demonstrate active listening by nodding and delivering pertinent responses.

8. Mock Interview Techniques:**The Mirror Technique**: Practice speaking in front of a mirror to observe your facial expressions and body language.

- **Video Recordings:** Record your practice sessions to go over your responses and check for ums, ahs and other filler words.
- **Speed and Clarity:** Ensure that you speak at an understandable pace and enunciate clearly.

9. Post-Interview: ****Thank You Note**
Send a personalised thank-you email within 24
hours of the interview, confirming your interest
in the role and reflecting on a subject raised
during the conversation.

10. Mental Preparation - **Stay Calm:**
Practice strategies to stay calm, such as deep
breathing or visualisation.

   - **Positivity:** Maintain a cheerful attitude
despite your nervousness.

11. Review and Reflect: After each
interview, consider what went well and what
didn't. Use this to make future improvements.

**12. Technical Preparation (for technical
positions)**technological Questions:** Prepare
to answer questions and solve problems relating
to your technological skills.

- **Coding Interviews:** If applicable, practise coding on a whiteboard or using a coding interview platform.

13. Realism - Recognise that even with thorough preparation, interviews may not result in a job offer. Use each experience as a stepping stone to further your progress.

Remember, practice is essential. It helps you develop your responses, boosts your confidence, and alleviates nervousness. Also, always strive to personalise your preparation to the exact job and organisation you're interviewing with.

- Follow-Up and Thank You Notes.

Certainly! Follow-up and thank-you notes are basic yet effective communication tools that are commonly utilised in both professional and personal settings. They can help to build a connection, express gratitude, and keep lines of contact open for future opportunities. Here is a full breakdown of each.

Follow-up notes:

1. **Purpose:** - Remind the receiver of earlier interactions or conversations.

   - To demonstrate ongoing interest in a work position, project, or opportunity.

   - To inquire about the current status of a previously discussed topic.

   - Provide any additional information that was required or that you neglected to mention.

   - Keep your name and qualifications at the top of the recipient's mind.

2. **Timing:** - Send a follow-up note within 24-48 hours of the meeting or interview.

- If it is a job application, follow up one to two weeks after sending it or after an interview if you have not received a response.

3. **Structure:** - **Greeting:** Address the recipient respectfully and professionally.

- **Opening:** Thank them for attending the meeting, interview, or chat.

- **Body:** Refer to specific points from your engagement. Reiterate your interest and briefly explain why you're a good fit if it's a job.
- **Action Item:** If applicable, specify what you are looking for (status update, second meeting, etc.).

- **Closing:** Finish with a respectful signature and your name.

- **Contact Information:** Make your contact information easy to find.

4. **Tone:** - Maintain a professional yet approachable tone.
   - Maintain a good attitude and demonstrate excitement and curiosity.

5. **Medium:** - Email is the preferred medium, however a phone call can be used for urgent instances.

Thank You Notes:

1. **Purpose:** - Express gratitude for a gift, time, support, or opportunity.
   - Make a positive and enduring impression.

2. **Timing:** - Send a thank-you note within 24 hours following the event or help.

3. **Structure:** - **Greeting:** A personalised address to the recipient.

   - **Opening:** A simple thank you.

- **Body:** Explain what specific gift or action you are grateful for and how it affected you.

- **concluding:** Express your gratitude and offer a pleasant concluding message.

- **Signature:** Please sign off with your name and contact details.

4. **Tone:** Be real and warm. It is critical to be authentic while thanking others.

- **Make it brief but meaningful.**

5. **Medium:** - Can be conveyed via email, handwritten message, or card, depending on the circumstance. Handwritten notes provide a personal touch to important acts of kindness or presents.

Both types of letters serve as etiquette tools for cultivating personal ties and improving professional connections. They demonstrate your

attention to detail and dedication to maintaining
courteous and caring communication.

Chapter 8

: Financial Literacy and Management**.

Financial literacy entails understanding money: how to earn, save, manage, and invest it properly. It's vital for making sound financial decisions. Meanwhile, financial management is the practical use of this knowledge in your daily life to budget, pay off debt, and accumulate wealth over time.

Here's a simple way to consider both:

1. **Financial Literacy:** Understanding the basics of money.

   - **Budgeting**: Keeping track of your income and expenses so you can plan your spending.

   - **Saving** means putting money aside for future needs or emergencies.

   - **Investing**: Using money to purchase assets that may increase in value over time.

   - **Credit**: Understanding how to use credit cards and loans prudently while maintaining a decent credit score.

   - **Insurance**: Protecting against financial risks such as illness or accidents.

2. **Financial Management:** Applying the ABCs in real life.

- **Planning**: Deciding what you want to do with your money, how much to save, and where to invest it.

- **Staying Disciplined**: Sticking to a budget and avoiding overspending.

- **Being Informed**: Monitoring financial news and making changes to your plan as needed.

- **Planning for the Future**: Consistently saving for long-term goals such as retirement or your children's schooling.

In essence, financial literacy provides the skills, whereas financial management is the constant process of creating and sustaining a healthy financial life using those resources.

- Budgeting for Teens

Teen budgeting is all about managing money effectively in order to balance savings, expenses, and even long-term investments. Let us break it down into simple steps.

Step 1: Understand Your Income.

First, calculate out how much money is coming in. This could stem from:

- Part-time job with weekly or monthly allowance.

- Earn money through odd tasks like babysitting or lawn mowing.

- Receive gifts for birthdays and holidays.

Step 2: Track Your Expenses

.Start tracking everything you spend money on. Expenses usually include:

- Meals and snacks
- Movie tickets or streaming service subscriptions.
- Petrol or public transport costs
- Clothing and phone bills.
- Other routine purchases.

Step 3: Set Goals

Consider your short- and long-term savings goals.

- Short-term: A new video game, concert tickets, or clothing.
- Long-term: Saving for a car, college money, or a major trip.

Step 4: Create a Budget Plan

Make a budget based on your income and expenses.Here's what you can add:

1. Fixed Expenses: These are fixed costs, such as subscription services or monthly phone bills.

2. Variable Expenses: These expenses can vary, including dining out, entertainment, and personal expenditures.

3. **Savings:** Decide how much you want to save each month for your goals.

4. **Emergency fund:** It's also a good idea to set aside some money for unforeseen expenses, such as repairing your bike or replacing a lost item.

Step 5: Prioritise Your Spending.

Decide what's most essential to you. If you want to save money for a car, you may want to limit your eating out.

Step 6: Use Budgeting Tools

Use tools to help you:

- Teen-friendly budgeting apps - Spreadsheets - Simple notebook for tracking income and expenses.

Step 7: Track and Adjust Your Budget

Monitor your progress on a regular basis:

- Are you remaining inside your spending budget?
- Do you need to change your savings goals?
- If you overspend, think out how to balance it out the next month.

Step 8: Learn and Improve.

The more you budget, the better you will become at it. Learn from your experiences.

- Determine what works and doesn't.
- To stay within your budget, you may have to make some compromises, such as skipping a movie night.

Step 9: Improve Your Financial Knowledge

Begin learning more about:

- Understand basic financial principles, such as interest rates and inflation. - Learn how to invest intelligently, even with tiny amounts of money. - Explore several savings accounts that can yield interest.

Step ten: Be consistent.

Stick to your budget and don't become disheartened if you encounter obstacles. Consistency is essential for developing excellent long-term financial habits.

For example, if you make $100 each month, you can set aside $40 for savings, $50 for spending, and $10 for an emergency fund.
- If you want to buy a $200 item, you will need to save $40 for five months, presuming you do not spend it on anything else.

Success Tips

: - **Be realistic:** Set spending that allow you to enjoy life without sacrificing savings.

- **Automate savings:** If possible, schedule an automatic transfer to your savings account as soon as you receive your paycheck.

- **Review and Adjust:** Life changes, and so does your budget. Check it every month.

Remember that budgeting is not about confining yourself; it is about giving you control over your finances. You may safeguard your financial future by following these procedures and tweaking them as you go.

Understanding Student Loans and Debt.

Student loans are a sort of financial aid that helps students pay for postsecondary education and related expenses such as tuition, books and supplies, and living expenses. Entering into a student loan agreement entails borrowing money, which you must repay with interest over time.

Understanding student loans and debt is crucial since they have a huge impact on your financial future. Here's a quick summary to help you comprehend the basics:

Types of Student Loans

1. **Federal Student Loan:** These government-backed loans typically feature lower interest rates and more flexible repayment choices than private loans. They consist of Direct Subsidised Loans, Direct Unsubsidized Loans, Direct PLUS Loans, and Federal Perkins Loans.

2. Private Student Loans: These are provided by banks, credit unions, and other private lenders. They are typically more expensive than federal loans and offer less flexible repayment choices.

Understanding Interest

- **Interest Rates:** The cost of borrowing money, calculated as a percentage of the loan amount. Federal loans typically have fixed interest rates, which means they do not alter over the term of the loan. Private loan rates might be fixed or variable.

Repayment Terms:

- **Grace Period:**. Many loans have a grace period after you leave school during which you are not required to make payments, though interest may still accrue.

- **Repayment Plan:** Federal loans provide a variety of repayment options, including standard, graduated, extended, income-driven, and others. Lenders will determine their own terms for private loans.

- **Term length:** This is the time period in which you will return the loan. Federal loans can last between 10 and 30 years, whereas private loans vary.

The Process of Taking Out A Student Loan

1) **FAFSA:** To apply for a federal loan, first fill out the Free Application for Federal Student Aid (FAFSA).

2. **Accepting a Loan:** If you are offered loans, you have the option of accepting them or deciding how much you need.

3. **Promissory Note:** By signing this paper, you agree to the terms of the loan.

Manage Your Debt

- **Budgeting:** Determine what you owe and build a budget that includes loan installments.

- **Prepayment:** If possible, pay more than the minimum payment or repay your loans early to save money on interest.

- **Loan Forgiveness:** Certain occupations are eligible for loan forgiveness programmes for federal loans.

- Consolidation and refinancing: You can combine numerous federal loans into one or refinance them with a private lender for a potentially lower interest rate.

Risks and Considerations

- **Overborrowing:** Only borrow what you need; remember that you will have to repay it with interest.

- **default:** Failure to repay your loan may result in default, which has serious ramifications for your credit score and financial future.

- **Credit Score Impact:** Your repayment history for student loans has an impact on your credit score. Late payments might lower your credit score, whereas repeated on-time payments will increase it.

Conclusion:

Before taking out a student loan, carefully review the terms and circumstances. Because government loans usually have better conditions, you should always look into them before considering private loans. Understanding your repayment options and responsibilities is critical to efficiently managing student debt and keeping it from becoming a lifelong burden.

- Saving and Investing

Saving and investing are two important strategies for money management and financial planning. I'll break down each topic into simple terms and explain how it works.

Saving.

What is savings?
Saving is setting aside money for later use rather than wasting it. Savings are often maintained in secure and easily accessible accounts, such as a bank savings account, so that you can access your money when needed.

Why save? - **Emergency Fund**: Life is unpredictable. Savings might help you cover unforeseen expenses such as auto repairs or medical bills.

- **Short-Term Goals**: Whether it's for a vacation, a new phone, or a down payment on a car, saving ensures you'll have the money when you need it.

- **Security**: Savings provide peace of mind knowing you have a financial cushion.

**How to Save?*

* - **Set Goals**: Determine your savings goal and amount needed.
-

Budget: Plan your monthly expenses to determine how much you can save.

- **Automate**: Make an automated transfer to your savings account every time you get paid.

- **Cut Expenses**: Look for ways to save money, such as eating out less or cancelling unnecessary subscriptions.

**Where to Save?*

* - **Bank Savings Account**: Ideal for short-term savings as they are secure and easily accessible.

• **Certificates of Deposit (CDs)** You can lock in your money for a certain amount of time by paying a little higher interest rate.

Investing

What is investment?

Investing is the process of putting money into assets that have the potential to increase in value over time, such as stocks, bonds, mutual funds, or real estate. The purpose of investing is to accumulate money over the long term.

Why Invest? - **Grow Wealth**: Investments can increase in value and provide larger returns than traditional savings accounts.

- **Retirement**: Investing is critical for retirement planning since it helps ensure that you have enough money to live on when you stop working.

- **Outpace Inflation**: Investments can grow faster than inflation, preserving your money's purchasing power.

How to Invest?

- **Research**: Determine your risk tolerance and explore various investing options.

- **diversification**: Spread your money across multiple investments to lessen risk.

- **The Long-Term Mindset**: Prepare to invest for years to withstand the market's ups and downs.

- **Expert Advice**: Consult a financial professional to assist design an investing strategy to your specific circumstances.
Q

Where to Invest?

- **Stocks**: Shares in corporations whose value fluctuates dependent on performance and market conditions.

- **Bonds**: Loans made to businesses or governments that earn you interest over time.

- **Mutual Funds** are collections of many types of investments handled by specialists.

- **Retirement Accounts (IRAs and 401(k)s)**: These accounts provide tax breaks for retirement savings.

Comparing Savings and Investing

Risk: Savings are normally low-risk, although they provide lesser returns. Investments can provide bigger profits, but they also carry a higher chance of loss.

Accessibility: Savings are easily available, however investments may be less liquid, which means you may not be able to withdraw your funds instantly or without penalty.

Purpose: Savings are intended to cover short-term expenses and emergencies.

Investments are for future goals, such as retirement, and can withstand market turbulence.

Growth Potential: Savings typically grow through interest, albeit at a low rate. Investments have the potential for compound growth, which means that your earnings can increase over time.

Saving and investing are both necessary components of a solid financial plan. You save to preserve and prepare for the short term, while investing to expand your money in the long run. The trick is to determine how much you should commit to each based on your financial condition, goals, and risk tolerance.

- Managing a Bank Account.

Managing a bank account does not need to be difficult. Here's a quick guide on how to do it efficiently:

1. Opening an Account:

- **Select the Right Bank:** Consider costs, interest rates, convenience, customer service, and internet access.

- **Decide on Account Types:** Savings to earn interest on deposits; checking for everyday transactions.

- **Provide Required Information:** Full name, address, contact information, identification, and sometimes a deposit.

2. **Understanding your account:**

- Keep track of your account balance. - Read the fine print to understand any costs for maintenance, overdrafts, or minimum balance restrictions.

- **Interest Rates:** If you have a savings account, understand the interest rate and how it is computed.

3. **Day-to-day Management:**

- **Use Online and Mobile Banking:** You can check your balance, pay bills and transfer funds between accounts electronically.

- **Track Transactions:** Review transactions on a regular basis to ensure accuracy and keep an eye out for fraudulent behaviour.

- **Set Up Alerts:** Be notified by text or email for specific activity, such as when your balance is low.

4. Budgeting:

- **Make a Budget:** Determine how much you'll spend and save each month.

- **Stick to Your Budget:** Use your account to monitor payments and stay on track with your budget.

5. **Saving money:**

- **Automatic Savings Plan:** Establish a monthly transfer from checking to savings account.

- **Emergency fund:** Try to save enough money to cover three to six months of living expenses.

6. **How to Avoid Fees and Charges:**

- **Overdraft Protection:** Consider setting this up to avoid overdraft penalties.

- **Minimum Balances:** To avoid fees, keep minimum balances in your account.

- **Use Your Bank's ATMs:** Avoid the costs that come with using other banks' ATMs.

7. Checking Statements:

- **Monthly Statements:** Check them for accuracy and understand your spending habits.

- **E-Statements:** Consider switching to electronic statements to decrease paper waste and maintain records easily accessible.

8. **Creating a Positive Relationship with Your Bank:**

- **Keep Your Contact Information Up To Date:** Ensure that the bank has your current address, phone number, and email address.

- **Communicate:** If you have any queries or concerns about your account, please contact customer service.

9. **Close an Account:**

- **Understanding the Process:** Some banks may demand a written notice or additional measures.

- Check for Fees or Penalties: Some accounts may incur closure fees or penalties if they are closed too soon after opening.

10. **Staying informed:**

- **Educate Yourself:** Take advantage of any financial literacy materials your bank provides.
Review Changes: Banks may change their policies, fees, or interest rates, so be informed of any developments.

By following these steps, you may manage your bank account in a simple and effective manner, keeping your money in order.

Chapter 9:

Health, Wellness, and Work-Life Balance.

In today's interconnected world, finding balance between our work, health, and overall well-being has become an essential component of living a fulfilling life. Health is our most valuable asset and the foundation of everything we do; it includes our physical, mental, and emotional states. Wellness is the proactive pursuit of activities, choices, and lifestyles that promote overall health. Together, health and wellness provide a framework for living an energised and fulfilling life.

Work-life balance is the art of balancing your professional and personal lives. It is the balance in which neither dominates the other and each receives the attention it deserves. Achieving this balance reduces stress, prevents burnout, and improves our quality of life. In essence, maintaining health, engaging in wellness, and seeking work-life balance are not luxuries, but rather necessary components of a happy, productive life.

- Stress Management.

Stress management entails taking control of your lifestyle, thoughts, emotions, and problem-solving strategies. Here is a simple guide that focuses on key areas of stress management.

Understand Stress

- **Identify triggers**: Recognize what makes you stressed. It could be work, family, change, or daily annoyances.

- **Accept your feelings**: Accept that stress is a response to something important to you, but that it should be temporary.

Lifestyle Changes

- **Regular exercise**: Physical activity can incrcase your endorphin levels. Try walking, swimming, or yoga.

- **Nutrition**: Eat a well-balanced diet. When your body is properly fueled, it can handle stress more effectively.

- **Sleep**: Aim for 7 to 9 hours per night. Quality sleep can help you feel better and think more clearly.

- Time Management: Prioritise tasks and avoid overcommitment. Break down large tasks into smaller steps.

Behavioural Techniques

- **Deep Breathing**: Counteract the stress response by taking slow, deep breaths from the diaphragm.

- **Progressive Muscle Relaxation**: Contract and then relax each muscle group to relieve physical tension.

- **Mindfulness Meditation**: Practice being present in the moment without judgement.

Cognitive Techniques.

- **Reframing thoughts**: Change your mindset and concentrate on positive or neutral thoughts.

- **Challenge beliefs**: Examine and modify any negative thought patterns.

Emotional Techniques

- **Express yourself**: Talk, laugh, cry, and express anger when necessary with someone you trust.

- **Pursue hobbies**: Make time for leisure activities that bring you joy.

Social Techniques

- **Connect with others**: Spend time with people who make you happy.

- **Set boundaries**: Learn to say no in a meaningful and respectful manner.

- **Seek support**: If stress becomes overwhelming, talk to your friends or seek professional help.

Professional Help

If stress is chronic or causes significant distress, Cognitive Behavioural Therapy (CBT) or counselling can help.

The Big Picture.

- **Acceptance**: Accept that some events are beyond your control.

- **Attitude**: Maintain a positive yet realistic attitude.
- **Perspective**: Stress is unavoidable in life. What matters is how you respond to it.

Remember that, while some stress is normal, feeling constantly overwhelmed is your body's way of telling you that you need to change your stress management strategy.

- Balancing School, Work, and Personal Life.

Many people struggle to balance their educational, professional, and personal lives. It entails creating a strategy, prioritising tasks, and being adaptable. Here are some simple strategies to help keep that balance.

1. **Create a Schedule:** - Make a weekly calendar.

- Set aside specific times for school, work, and personal activities.

- Stick to the schedule as closely as possible, but be prepared to adjust as needed.

2. **Prioritise Tasks:** Organize your tasks by importance and deadline.

- Start with high-priority tasks and work your way down to less critical ones.

3. **Use a Planner:** - Use a planner or digital app to manage assignments, work commitments, and personal events.

- Check and update it every day to avoid last-minute rushes or forgotten tasks.

4. Establish boundaries: - Communicate to friends, family, and employers when you are available and when you need to prioritise schoolwork.

- Learn to say "no" when you need to prioritise your tasks.

5. Avoid burnout by taking short breaks throughout the day to rest and recharge.
   - Do activities that you enjoy and that help you relax.

6. Maintain your physical health by exercising regularly, eating a balanced diet, and getting enough sleep.
   - Mental health is equally important, so use stress-reduction techniques such as meditation or deep breathing exercises.

7. **Be Efficient:** - Improve your study or work productivity.
   - This could include holding group study sessions or using productivity software.

8. Communicate: - Inform your teachers, employers, and family about your commitments.
- They can frequently provide assistance or adjustments to help you manage.

9. **Use Downtime Wisely:** - Use free periods at school or breaks at work to catch up on assignments or study.

10. **Appraise and Adjust:**

   - Evaluate your plan's effectiveness on a regular basis.

   - Adjust your schedule as your school, work, and personal commitments change.

Remember, balance does not imply doing everything at once. It's about making decisions that are consistent with your goals and responsibilities while not overwhelming yourself. Be kind to yourself throughout this process. If you find that balancing is too difficult, you may need to consider reducing your workload, whether at work, school, or in social activities.

- The Importance of Sleep, Exercise, and Nutrition.

Let us simplify the three essential pillars of health: sleep, exercise, and nutrition.

Sleep:

1. **Recovery:** While sleeping, your body repairs itself. This downtime allows your

muscles, organs, and various cells to recover from the day's activities.

2. **Brain Health:** Sleep functions as a reset button for your brain. It aids in the removal of waste and the reorganisation of day-old information. Good sleep can help with memory and learning.

3. **Emotional Balance:** When you sleep, your brain processes emotions. Getting enough sleep increases your chances of waking up with a stable mood and greater emotional resilience.

4. **Physical Health:** A good night's sleep is associated with a healthier heart, a stronger immune system, and a lower risk of obesity and diabetes.

5. **Performance:** After a good night's sleep, you should be more alert and have better concentration, decision-making abilities, and coordination.

Exercise:

1. **Strengthens the Body:** Regular exercise builds muscle strength and bone density. It improves endurance and muscle strength.

2. **Improves Mental Health:** Physical activity produces hormones like endorphins, which make you feel good. It can help to alleviate depression, stress, and anxiety.

3. **Improves Sleep:** Exercise can help you fall asleep faster and sleep deeper, as long as it isn't too close to bedtime.

4. **Reduces Disease Risk:** Physical activity can lower the risk of chronic diseases like heart disease, type 2 diabetes, and certain cancers.

5. **Weight Management:** Exercise burns calories, which is essential for maintaining a healthy weight or losing weight.

Nutrition:

1. **Energy Provision:** Food is fuel. Eating provides your body with the energy it requires to function normally.

2. **Building Blocks:** Nutrients from food are required for development and repair. They contribute to the development of muscle, bone, and other essential tissues.

3. **Disease Prevention:** A well-balanced diet can lower your risk of developing certain diseases, such as heart disease, stroke, or type 2 diabetes.

4. **Overall Health:** Good nutrition benefits all of your body's systems, including the immune and nervous systems, and contributes to overall health.

5. **Brain Function:** The brain requires nutrients just like the heart and muscles. Certain foods can enhance brain function by influencing mood, memory, and concentration.

Aligning Sleep, Exercise, and Nutrition:

- Visualise these three pillars as a tripod that supports your overall well-being. When one leg is shorter than the others, the tripod may still stand but will be wobbly and unstable.

- Getting into a routine can help. Set a regular bedtime, schedule physical activity, and plan nutritious meals.

- Small changes can have a large impact. You don't have to run marathons, sleep ten hours a night, or eat only salads. Begin with small changes, such as taking a brisk 20-minute walk, increasing your sleep by 30 minutes, and including more vegetables in your diet.

- Always remember to listen to your body. It usually understands what it needs. Take a break if you're tired. If you are sedentary, get moving.

If you're eating poorly, make a change to your diet.

Keeping it simple—get enough sleep, stay active, and eat a well-balanced diet. These actions complement each other and can significantly improve your quality of life.

- Mental Health Resources.

Caring for one's mental health is as important as looking after physical health. There are various resources available to help people cope with mental health issues. Here's a simple guide to understanding some of the most common mental health resources:

1. **Counseling and Therapy**
- **What it is:** Professional support from licensed therapists or counselors who listen and help you work through personal challenges.

- **How to find:** Seek referrals from your doctor, search online directories, contact insurance providers for covered therapists, or use therapy apps.

2. **Psychiatrists**

- **What it is:** Medical doctors specializing in mental health who can diagnose conditions and prescribe medications.

- **How to find:** Get a referral from your primary care physician or search through your health insurance network.

3. **Support Groups**

- **What it is:** Groups of people with similar mental health challenges meeting to discuss their experiences and support each other.

- **How to find:** Look for local community centers, hospitals, or research online for virtual groups.

4. **Crisis Helplines**

- **What it is:** Immediate and confidential support over the phone or text, often available 24/7.
- **Examples:** National Suicide Prevention Lifeline, Crisis Text Line.

- **How to use:** Call or text when in urgent need of someone to talk to.

5. **Online Mental Health Platforms**

- **What it is:** Websites or apps offering therapy and counseling services over the internet.

- **How to find:** Search for reputable online therapy services and check their reviews.

6. **Mental Health Apps**

- **What it is:** Mobile applications designed to help with various aspects of mental health, like reducing anxiety, helping with sleep, or tracking mood.

- **How to use:** Download from app stores and follow in-app guidance.

7. **Community Mental Health Centers**

- **What it is:** Local centers providing mental health services on a sliding fee scale.

- **How to find:** Check the government's health department website or search for centers in your area.

8. **Hospital Psychiatric Departments**

- **What it is:** Hospitals may have specialized units for mental health care, providing comprehensive services.

- **How to find:** Research hospitals nearby to see if they have such units and understand their services.

9. **Books and Educational Resources**

- **What it is:** Literature aimed at understanding and coping with mental health issues.
- **How to find:** Libraries, bookstores, or online platforms; seek recommendations from therapists.

10. **School and University Counseling Services**

- **What it is:** Education institutions often provide students with free or low-cost mental health services.

- **How to access:** Contact your institution's health center or student services.

11. **Employee Assistance Programs (EAP)**

- **What it is:** Programs through employers that offer free and confidential assessments, counseling, and referrals for employees.

- **How to access:** Contact your Human Resources department for information.

12. **Self-Care Practices**

- **What it is:** Personal activities that promote well-being, such as meditation, exercise, and proper sleep.

- **How to practice:** Incorporate activities that you enjoy and that are beneficial for your mental health into your daily routine.

13. **Educational Workshops and Seminars**

- **What it is:** Sessions that provide information and teach strategies for managing mental health.

- **How to find:** Look for announcements at community centers, libraries, or healthcare providers.

Key Considerations When Seeking Help:

- **Quality and Credentials:** Ensure that the providers are licensed and have good reviews or testimonials.

- **Cost:** Consider what you can afford; many services offer sliding-scale fees based on income.

- **Privacy:** Understand how your information will be kept confidential.

- **Comfort Level:** It's important that you feel comfortable and safe with the mental health professional or service.

- **Accessibility:** Consider how easily you can access the service (location, online, hours of operation).

It's okay to ask for help, and it's okay to try out different resources until you find the right fit for your needs. Your mental health is a priority, and taking the step to explore these resources is already a big move toward self-care.

**Chapter 10:

Navigating the Transition from Teen to Adult**.

Entering adulthood is like entering a new world; it is a transition from the familiar routines of adolescence to a vast landscape of opportunities and responsibilities. As teenagers say goodbye to their high school years, they welcome a future that will be shaped by their own decisions and actions. This transition, while exciting, can be both daunting and momentous.

Because everyone's journey is unique, there is no manual for navigating this transition. However, there are some shared signposts and milestones along the way. Emerging adults face a slew of life-altering decisions, ranging from learning to manage finances and making career choices to maintaining healthy relationships and understanding one's identity.

This transition period lays the groundwork for a future that will be proudly remembered. It's time to ask questions, seek guidance, and embrace the knowledge that comes with each new step. So, let's turn the page and begin to investigate what it means to confidently step from the familiar shores of adolescence into the vast ocean of maturity.

- The Reality of Adulthood Responsibilities.

Adulthood responsibilities can be a difficult transition from the carefree days of youth. As we enter adulthood, we are confronted with new levels of expectations, legal obligations, and social pressures that necessitate mature responses. Here is an example of what these responsibilities look like:

1. Financial Independence: One of the most important indicators of adulthood is the ability to manage one's own finances. This includes budgeting, timely bill payment, debt management, and future savings. An adult is expected to make their own money through work or entrepreneurship and spend it wisely.

2. Employment: Securing a stable job not only provides financial independence, but it also helps to shape one's identity and self-esteem. Adults are expected to work unless they are unable to do so due to disability or retirement.

3. Housing and Domestic Skills: Adults are responsible for keeping a living space clean, whether they rent a flat, own a home or simply keep a room tidy. They must also be capable of handling tasks such as cooking, cleaning, and laundry on their own.

4. Health and Personal Care: Adults must be responsible for their own health, which includes scheduling and attending doctor's appointments, living a healthy lifestyle, and managing health-related finances like insurance and medical bills.

5. Relationships and Social Life: Adulthood entails developing and maintaining relationships, which range from friendships and romantic partnerships to professional networks. This includes improving interpersonal skills and emotional intelligence.

6. Legal responsibilities: Adults are completely responsible for their actions in the eyes of the law. They must understand and follow societal rules and regulations, including civic responsibilities such as voting and jury duty.

7. Long-term planning: As an adult, you should plan for your future, which includes career advancement, retirement savings, investing, and possibly starting a family.

8. Crisis Management. Adults are expected to manage emergencies and crises responsibly. This could range from a medical emergency to a sudden job loss, and it necessitates the ability to think on one's feet and respond quickly.

9) Self-reflection and Growth: This responsibility entails being aware of one's own strengths and weaknesses, constantly learning and adapting in order to become a well-rounded individual.

10. Community Involvement: Many adults feel compelled to give back to their communities, whether by volunteering, participating in local politics, or simply being a good neighbour.

These responsibilities may appear daunting, but they are a natural part of growing up and are typically met gradually as people gain experience and confidence. Facing these responsibilities head on with a proactive and positive attitude can lead to a more fulfilling and independent life.

Rights and Legal Issues for Young Adults.

When young adults reach a certain age, which in many countries is typically 18, they gain new legal rights and responsibilities. Here are key points that summarise some of these rights and legal issues in a straightforward manner:

1. **Age of Majority** - **Definition:** The legal adult age.

- **Why it matters:** You can make legal decisions for yourself, enter into contracts, and be held fully accountable for your actions.

- **Example:** At 18, you can sign a flat lease agreement without the need for a parent or guardian to cosign.

2: **Voting**What it is:** The ability to vote.

- **Why it's important:** As a young adult, your vote has the potential to influence local, state, and national politics.

- Here's an example: When you reach the age of majority, you can register to vote and participate in the upcoming election.

3. **Employment** - **Definition:** The right to work and earn a wage.

- **Why it matters:** You are entitled to fair labour practices, a minimum wage, and, in some cases, worker rights.

- Here's an example: As a legal adult, you can work full-time and are eligible for a wider range of jobs.

4: **Privacy and Personal Rights*

*What it is:** Rights that protect your privacy and autonomy.

- **Why it matters:** You have more privacy rights, including medical confidentiality.

- Here's an example: Your health records are private, and parents can no longer view them without your permission.

5. **Healthcare Decisions**

- **What it is:** The right to accept or refuse medical treatment.

- **Why it matters:** You have control over your body and health decisions.

- Here's an example: You can choose which medical treatments or surgeries you want to have.

6: **Financial Independence*

*What it entails:** The ability to open bank accounts and manage finances independently.

 - **Why it matters:** You can establish credit, apply for loans, and make investments.

 - For example, you can apply for a credit card or a loan without the need for a parent or guardian.

7: **Legal Responsibility**

What it is: **Being held legally accountable for your actions.

 - **Why it matters:** You are legally liable for any contracts you make or crimes you commit.

 - **Example:** If you receive a traffic ticket, you must pay the fine or contest it in court.

8. **Education and Student Rights**

- **Definition:** Rights related to education and student status.

- **Why it matters: **You have specific educational rights, such as record privacy and the right to an education.

- For example, if you have a disability, you can manage your educational loans and request accommodations.

9. **Marriage and Family**

- **What it is:** The right to marry and start a family. - **Why it matters:** You can legally enter into a marriage and make decisions about family planning.

- For example, at 18, you can marry without parental consent in most places.

10. **Military Service*

* - **What it is:** The opportunity to join the military.

- **Why it matters:** You can choose to serve your country, which may include educational or professional benefits.

- For example, you can enlist in the armed forces without parental approval.

11. **Legal Proceedings*

* - **What it is:** The right to be tried in court as an adult.

- **Why it matters:** As an adult, you face the legal system, which can result in harsher penalties but also greater rights.

- **Example:** If you are accused of a crime, you are entitled to a fair trial and legal representation.

12. **Civic Responsibilities**

- **What it is:** Community-based responsibilities.

- **Why it matters:** You contribute to society by obeying the law, serving on juries, and paying taxes.

- **For example:** When you reach the age of majority, you may be called to jury duty.

Tips for Navigating Rights and Legal Issues: -

Educate Yourself: Research your rights and responsibilities through legal websites, government resources, or civic classes.

- **Seek Guidance:** When making major decisions, do not be afraid to seek legal advice from trusted professionals.

- **Plan Ahead:** Think about your long-term goals and how your decisions, particularly those involving finances and contracts, will align with them.

It is critical to remember that, while reaching the age of majority confers many rights, it also entails a set of responsibilities and potential legal ramifications for your actions. Knowing your rights and preparing for adult responsibilities will help you navigate young adulthood more successfully.

- Finding Mentors and Advisers.

Finding mentors and advisers can be a critical step towards both personal and professional development. Here's a straightforward guide on how to do this:

Understanding Your Needs:

Before seeking a mentor or adviser, define your goals. Are you looking for career advice, skill development, networking opportunities, or industry insights?

Identify Potential Mentors:

1. **Professional Networks**: Look within your existing professional network for former bosses, experienced colleagues, or industry contacts.

2. **Online Platforms**: Search LinkedIn, Twitter, or industry-specific forums for professionals who share your interests.

3. **Mentoring Programmes**: Several organisations and universities provide formal mentoring programmes.

4. **Events and Conferences**: Attend industry conferences, workshops, and

networking events to connect with potential mentors in person.

5. **Social Groups**: Look for local clubs, associations, or community groups that are relevant to your interests.

Reach Out Effectively:

1. **Initial Contact**: A brief, courteous email or message is frequently the best first step. Introduce yourself, express your admiration for their work, and explain why you're reaching out.

2. **Be Specific**: Mention specific challenges or goals you're working towards that you believe the mentor can assist with.

3. **Request a Meeting**: Ask if they'd be interested in a brief meeting—a coffee chat or a quick phone call is often a low-pressure option.

Prepare for the meeting:

1. **Do Your Homework**: To ensure a productive conversation, research your potential mentor's background, work, and interests.

2. **Set Clear Objectives**: Know what you want from the meeting. Prepare questions to help you determine whether this person is a good fit as a mentor or adviser.

3. **Respect Their Time**: Arrive on time for the meeting, stay within the time frame agreed upon, and express gratitude for their willingness to meet.

Establishing the Relationship:

1. **Mutual Benefit**: Recognise that mentoring should not be one-sided. Offer your own skills or assistance in exchange.

2. **Set Expectations**: Be clear about the type of guidance you seek and how frequently you want to communicate.

3. **Formal Agreement**: In some cases, particularly in a professional setting, it may be beneficial to formalise the mentor-mentee relationship through an agreement outlining goals and commitments.

Maintaining the Relationship:

1. **Regular Check-Ins**: Keep in touch with your mentor on the agreed-upon schedule, whether weekly, monthly, or quarterly.

2. **Show Appreciation**: Always thank them for their time and advice.

3. **Provide Updates**: Share your progress with your mentor; this shows them the value they're adding and encourages them to keep supporting you.

4. **Be Open to Feedback**: An effective mentor will offer constructive criticism. Pay close attention and apply what you learn.

5. **Reciprocate**: If you have the opportunity to help your mentor or provide support in any way, do so.

Developing the Relationship:

Your needs may change over time, as will the nature of the mentor-mentee relationship. It can lead to a lifelong friendship or a professional partnership. Be open to the relationship's natural progression.

To summarise, finding mentors and advisers entails recognising your needs, identifying potential mentors, reaching out effectively, establishing clear communication, maintaining the relationship, and remaining open to its evolution over time. Simple and respectful interactions are frequently the key to establishing and maintaining these valuable relationships.

**Chapter 11

Looking Ahead**

As we stand on the verge of today, the horizon of tomorrow spreads out before us, full of the promise of the unknown and the excitement of possibility. "Looking Ahead" is more than just catching a glimpse of the future; it is about preparing for it, understanding the seeds we plant today that will blossom into the realities of tomorrow. In these pages, we'll go on a journey—a thoughtful exploration of what lies ahead, the innovations that are waiting to be realised, and the dreams that call us forward. So take a deep breath and let's walk into the future together, eyes wide open and hearts ready for the adventure that lies ahead.

- Career Advancement and Continuing Education.

Career advancement is the process of moving up the ranks in your job or field, which often entails gaining higher-level positions, more responsibility, and higher pay. Continuing education is when you continue to learn and develop your skills after you have completed your formal education, usually to advance your career. Here is a simple breakdown:

Career advancement:

1. Set goals for your career. This could be a higher position, a different type of work, or specialising in a specific field.

2. **Gaining Experience:** - Participate in projects that enhance your skills and experience. Demonstrate that you can handle responsibility and produce results.

3. Networking: - Connect with professionals in your field. They can provide advice, mentorship, or inform you about new job opportunities.

4. **Performance:** - Perform well at your current job. Being recognised for good work can result in promotions or recommendations.

5. **Visibility:** - Ensure your work is seen by others. This could include giving presentations, reports, or leading meetings.

6. **Job Search Skills:** - Develop effective resume and cover letter writing skills. Prepare for interviews and learn how to negotiate offers.

Continuing education:

1. **Formal Education:** This includes relevant degree programmes, certificates, professional designations, or diplomas.

2. **Online Courses:** - Numerous platforms offer courses in diverse fields. They range from short tutorials to full-length university courses.

3. Professional Development Workshops: Employers, professional bodies, and training companies frequently provide these services. They help you stay up to date in your field.

4. **Self-Directed Learning:** - Reading books, researching online, practicing new skills, or gaining knowledge from colleagues.

5. Attending conferences and seminars can provide valuable insights into your field and facilitate networking opportunities.

6. **Licencing and Certifications:** - Certain professions require ongoing education to maintain licences or certificates. This ensures that your expertise is recognised and valid.

When you combine career advancement strategies with continuing education, you have a better chance of success in your field. Employers frequently value employees who are proactive about learning and willing to take on additional responsibilities. It demonstrates that you are dedicated to your career and eager to improve.

Navigating the Job Market Post-College.

Navigating the job market after college can be a challenging but rewarding experience. Here's a simple guide to completing this phase:

Step 1: Assess Skills and Interests
- **Identify Your Strengths:** Consider what you excel at. These could be skills you developed in college or even hobbies.

- **Understand Your Interests:** Consider the subjects or activities that interest you. It is critical to enjoy what you will be doing.

282

- **Evaluate your values:** What is important to you in your job? Location? Work-life balance? What about company culture?

Step 2: Resume and Online Presence

- Tailor your resume to highlight relevant experience, academic projects, and skills for the job you're applying for.

- **Create a LinkedIn Profile:** Make sure your profile is up-to-date and matches your resume. Connect with alumni, classmates, and professionals.

- **Cleaning Up Social Media:** Employers may review your social media presence. Make sure it represents you professionally.

Step 3: Research and Exploration

- **Industry Research:** Identify industries that match your interests and skills.

283

- **Job Roles:** Research various roles in these industries to see what suits you.

- **Networking**: Attend job fairs, join professional organisations, and contact alumni for informational interviews.

Step 4: Application Process

- **Apply Widely**: Send applications to multiple companies. Use job search sites like Indeed, Glassdoor, and LinkedIn.

- **Customise Cover Letters:** For each application, write a unique cover letter that expresses your interest in the position and the company.

- **Tracking Applications:** Keep a spreadsheet to track your applications and follow-up dates.

Step 5: Interview Preparation

- **Research Companies:** Prior to interviews, learn about the company's culture, values, and recent news.

- **Practice Interviewing:** Hold mock interviews with friends or use online resources to practice common questions.

- **Prepare Questions:** Create a list of questions about the role and company to ask the interviewer.

Step 6: The Interview

- **Dress Appropriately:** Ensure your attire aligns with the company's culture, whether business professional or casual.
- **Arrive Early:** Plan on arriving 10-15 minutes early to allow for any unexpected delays.

- **Body Language:** Be aware of nonverbal communication—eye contact, a firm handshake, and good posture convey confidence.

Step 7: After the Interview

- **Send a Thank You Note:** Send a thank-you email within 24 hours, expressing gratitude for the opportunity.

- **Reflect:** Consider what worked well and what could be improved for the next time.

- **Be patient.** Hiring can be slow. While you are waiting for a response, continue to apply for other positions.

Step 8: Evaluating Offers

- **Compare Offers:** When receiving multiple offers, consider your values, desired salary, benefits, growth potential, and location.

- Negotiate: Don't be afraid to negotiate your starting salary and other benefits.

Step 9: Continuous Learning

- **Skill Development:** Learn new skills related to your field through online courses, workshops, or readings.

- **Professional Networking:** Continue to grow your network. Maintaining relationships may lead to future employment opportunities.

Step 10: Transition to Professional Life

- **Set Expectations:** Recognise that your first job may not be your dream job, but rather a stepping stone in your career.

- **Adapt to Workplace Culture:** Be willing to accept the norms and practices of your new workplace.

- **Seek Feedback:** To improve your performance, seek feedback on a regular basis.

Navigating the job market after college is an iterative process that requires constant self-improvement, perseverance, and a willingness to step outside of your comfort zone. While everyone's journey is unique, these steps provide a general framework to help you navigate your professional career.

- Entrepreneurship as a Career Path

Entrepreneurship as a career path involves pursuing an opportunity to start a new business or venture, innovate existing products or services, or develop novel solutions to problems. It's a path that involves taking financial risks in the hopes of profiting, but it also has the potential for personal fulfilment, autonomy, and, in some cases, significant financial rewards. Here's a straightforward look at entrepreneurship as a career path:

1. Identifying Opportunities:
Entrepreneurs are people who are good at identifying market gaps or problems that need to be solved. This could include developing a new product, providing a service that does not currently exist in a specific location, or improving on what is already available.

****2. Innovation.****
Entrepreneurship is fundamentally based on innovation. This includes not only coming up with new ideas, but also determining how to effectively implement them. Entrepreneurs must be able to think creatively and translate their ideas into marketable products or services.

****3. Plan:****
Starting a business requires meticulous planning. Entrepreneurs must create a business plan outlining their idea, market analysis, sales strategy, funding requirements, and long-term objectives. This strategy is critical for both

guiding the startup and persuading potential investors or lenders to provide funding.

4. Financial Risk: Starting a business requires an initial investment. Entrepreneurs typically invest their own money, seek loans, or pitch investors for funding. They must be willing to accept that the business may fail and that they will lose their invested capital.

5) Perseverance:
Entrepreneurship is challenging. It frequently includes long hours, setbacks, and failures. Entrepreneurs must be resilient and determined to persevere even when times are tough. Perseverance is essential for overcoming obstacles and reaching success.

6. Flexible and Adaptable:
The market changes quickly, and businesses must be adaptable in order to survive. Entrepreneurs must be adaptable, willing to tweak their business model, adapt to new trends, or pivot their business as needed.

7. Independence.

Many people choose entrepreneurship because of the independence it provides. Entrepreneurs make their own decisions and steer their businesses in the direction they believe is best. The ability to be your own boss is a major draw.

8. Leadership and Management:

As a company grows, entrepreneurs must develop leadership and management skills. They will need to hire employees, manage a team, and lead their company to achieve its goals.

9. Learning and Personal Development:

Entrepreneurs are continuous learners. They learn from their mistakes and successes, and they are always looking for ways to improve themselves personally and professionally. Each challenge represents an opportunity to learn something new.

10. Potential Financial Rewards:

While the financial risk is high, the potential rewards are substantial. If a business succeeds, an entrepreneur can earn a substantial income and, perhaps more importantly, a sense of personal accomplishment.

11. Contribution to Society:

Many entrepreneurs are motivated by the desire to make a positive contribution to the world. They can use their businesses to introduce products or services that improve people's lives, create jobs, and help the economy grow.

12: Uncertain Path

It is important to remember that there is no guarantee of success in entrepreneurship. The path is uncertain and may be unpredictable. The risk and the unknown are constant companions on the entrepreneurial path.

In summary, entrepreneurship is a career path for those who are creative, self-sufficient, resilient, and willing to take risks. It can be rewarding and potentially profitable, but it necessitates hard work, dedication, and the ability to learn from both mistakes and successes. Many people find this path rewarding not only financially, but also personally, because it allows them to create something new and valuable.

- Lifelong Learning and Skills Development.

Lifelong learning and skill development are two interconnected concepts that revolve around a person's ongoing pursuit of knowledge and abilities, regardless of age or professional status. Let us break down the two:

Lifelong Learning:

Lifelong learning is the continuous, voluntary, and self-motivated pursuit of knowledge for a variety of reasons, including personal and professional development, social inclusion, active citizenship, and other personal fulfilment. It can occur in a variety of settings, ranging from formal education institutions such as schools and universities to more informal settings such as the home, workplace, or community activities. Here are some key points that explain lifelong learning in plain terms:

- **Continual Process**: Learning is an ongoing process.

- **Self-Driven**: The individual's desire and goals motivate them to learn.

- **Diverse Sources**: Learning can occur through books, online courses, workshops, seminars, and everyday experiences.

- **Benefits Beyond Jobs**: In addition to career advancement, it enriches one's personal life and contributes to a well-rounded society.

Skill Development:

Skills development is concerned with the acquisition and improvement of skills required for the workplace, personal development, or hobbyist activities. This can include improving existing skills or learning new ones in order to remain relevant in a rapidly changing world. Skills can be technical, such as programming or machine repair, or soft, such as communication, leadership, and problem solving. Here are some important aspects:

- **Workplace Relevance**: Frequently associated with increased job performance or career advancement.

- **Formal and Informal Learning**: Can be obtained through structured courses or on-the-job training.

- **Adaptability**: Assists individuals in responding to changes in their industry or occupation.

- **Skillset Diversity**: Promotes a more adaptable skill set, which can lead to new opportunities.

How They Connect:

1. **Adaptivity in a Changing World**: Both are concerned with keeping up with changes in technology, societal needs, and the labour market. As industries evolve, the skills in demand change, emphasising the importance of continuous learning.

2. **Professional Competitiveness**: Lifelong learning and skill development can increase a person's competitiveness in the job market, allowing them to secure promotions or new opportunities.

3. **Personal Growth**: They promote broad personal development, resulting in richer lives

and allowing people to interact with the world in a more informed and competent manner.

4. **Economic Benefits**: On a broader scale, they help with economic adaptation and growth, as a skilled and knowledgeable workforce is a valuable asset in any economy.

Implementing Lifelong Learning and Skill Development:

- **Set Goals**: Determine what you want to achieve, whether it's career advancement, personal interests, or simply keeping up with current trends.

- **Explore Resources**: Utilise online resources, community colleges, libraries, and free webinars.

- **Make a Plan**: Make a learning schedule that works for your lifestyle and stick to it.

- **Stay curious**: Always keep an eye out for new things to learn.

- **Apply What You Learn**: Put your new skills and knowledge to use, whether at work or on a personal project.

To summarise, lifelong learning and skill development entails maintaining a curious and open mindset throughout one's life while constantly building and updating one's skill set in order to remain relevant, fulfilled, and effective in a changing world.

Conclusion

Starting your journey to college and a career is like standing at the edge of a vast forest. The path you choose today can take you through a landscape of opportunities and experiences that will shape your future self. As a teenager at this critical juncture, remember that you are the cartographer of your own map, drawing lines from your dreams to reality. Encouragement will guide you on this journey, while determination will propel you forward.

To begin, recognise that planning for college and career is a sign of your maturing perspective, a salute to the responsibility you're prepared to accept. Accept the challenge with a brave heart and a mind eager to learn. You will face times of uncertainty and difficult decision-making, but remember that every seasoned professional was once a beginner. Encouragement comes not only from others, but also from within. Trust in yourself and the abilities you've acquired along the way.

The world of college and career planning is vast, and your decisions are important—but not irreversible. Remember that flexibility is essential to success. As you grow, your interests and goals may change. Allow yourself the flexibility and courage to change course if your heart or intellect leads you down a different path. Reassessing and realigning your goals demonstrates wisdom, not weakness.

Create a network of support that includes teachers, counsellors, family members, and mentors who believe in you. Allow them to be your sounding boards and cheerleaders. Furthermore, look for stories from others who have walked this path before you. Their experiences can serve as lighthouses, guiding you away from common shoals and pitfalls.

While academics are an important part of college preparation, personal development is equally important. Participate in activities that promote leadership, empathy, and teamwork. Skills acquired in these areas are invaluable and frequently distinguish good candidates from great ones.

Remember that there are several paths to a rewarding career. College is one option, but vocational training, entrepreneurship, and direct entry into the workforce are all viable options. Your journey should reflect your strengths and passions, not societal expectations.

As you move forward, keep in mind that every effort you make today contributes to the foundation of your future. It is natural to feel overwhelmed at times, but never underestimate the distance that can be travelled with small, consistent steps. Set goals that are challenging but attainable with determination and hard work.

Finally, believe in your ability to learn and excel. You possess a one-of-a-kind set of skills and goals that the world is eager to see. Your college and career planning journey is about more than just occupational titles and degrees; it is about discovering who you are and who you want to be.

Take heart, traveller. The path ahead is full of opportunity and promise, and you are more than prepared to navigate its twists and turns. Step forward with confidence and curiosity, because your story is just beginning.

I HAVE A REQUEST

Dear friend,

Your support as a reader has been the cornerstone of my writing journey. Following my Author Central page is more than just staying updated—it's about being a part of a community that celebrates the magic of literature together.To follow, simply visit https://www.amazon.com/author/feliciatree], and click 'Follow' button beneath my profile photo. It's that easy! Or scan

Thank you for your support and happy reading!

Warmest regards,

[Felicia Tree]

Additional Resources.

Hello, please if you found this book valuable, kindly check out my other book. Thank you very much for your support.

Procrastination's Worst Enemy:

A Practical Guide to Mastering Time Management and unleashed success in life and work. By Felicia Tree